AF573687

A Silver Shape

'A silver shape like his early love doth pass.'

SHELLEY: *The Two Voices*

A Silver Shape

Recollections of a Victorian Romance

by

George Crawshay

Edited and Illustrated by

Edmund Esdaile

Athenaeum with Frederick Muller

This edition first published 1980 by
The Athenaeum Publishing Co Ltd
and distributed throughout the world by
Frederick Muller Ltd, Victoria Works,
Edgware Road, London, NW2 6LE

ISBN 0–584–10499–5

British Library Cataloguing in Publication Data

Crawshay, George
A silver shape.
1. Country life – England – Midlands
2. Midlands – Social life and customs
I. Title II. Esdaile, Edmund
942.4′081′0924 S522.G7

Set and printed in Great Britain by
Clarke, Doble & Brendon Ltd, Plymouth and London

To My Friends

Myles Thoroton Hildyard

and

Henry Thorold

from

Their "Honorary Cousin"

E.E.

Contents

Illustrations

Editor's Preface

I am glad to have had this opportunity of rescuing George Crawshay from oblivion. In the following pages is recorded an intimate episode in his early life which only a person with the charm born of an inner grace could have so written. He was a man of varied distinction and it is satisfying therefore to me as editor that it has been possible, without irrelevance, to include in the postscript and notes incidental allusions which, added to certain details in the main text, reveal some of the author's manifold qualities. Only last autumn did I hear of his family's generous and sustained benefactions to the Royal Free Hospital.

E.E.

CHAPTER I

The Coronation Day

JUNE 28, 1838, is a day I have reason to remember.

At that date I was the sole resident pupil with a clergyman in a Midland county, who was preparing me for Cambridge. The Rectory was at the end of a short lane that led from the village to the Church. The Rectory garden opened into the churchyard, on the other side of which stood the Hall, a large brick building, one end looking into the churchyard, and having indeed the same wall. You could stretch your hand from the churchyard into the window of the housekeeper's room. From the Hall garden a door opened into the end of the lane, and a gate into the churchyard from the stableyard, which was of such dimensions as to contain a green large enough for a dance, and which was kept in suitable condition. This was indeed the village green. There was no other. The lane came to an end at the wall of the Hall garden, but led to a footpath, which, after traversing several fields in front of the park, came out into the London road, and on the other side of the park was a lane passing by the park lodge and connecting the London road with the village, which, together with some ten thousand acres of good land, belonged to the owners of the Hall.

The footpath and lane were each about a mile in length, and the points at which they joined the London road about half-a-mile distant. The village consisted of a few farmhouses, a few shops, and a good many labourer's cottages. Here was Church and State in miniature. Washington Irving's *Bracebridge Hall*, a tale with little incident, but much interesting description of English country life, such as it was at the time when this genial and sympathetic writer became acquainted with it, will give some idea of the medium in which I here found myself, allowance being made for the lapse of time, the period covered by *Bracebridge Hall* being a generation earlier than in 1838.

The incidents I have to relate can hardly have any interest excepting to myself. I shall relate them as truly as my memory, aided by some memoranda, will allow, for my own satisfaction and relief; but the reader may perhaps take some interest in a picture of English country life such as it was more than fifty years ago. I cannot hope to approach Washington Irving, but his example has influenced me in deciding to write. If I had never read *Bracebridge Hall*, I might never have attempted to narrate the uneventful episodes of my early love.

I arrived at the Rectory by travelling about a hundred miles from London outside a coach in the month of May. I had entered upon my eighteenth year, and, up to this date, my surroundings had been of a character quite opposite to those among which I now found myself. I was the eldest son of a gentleman belonging to one of those families of manufacturers which achieved greatness at the end of the last century. My father's wealth was considerable, although by no means what it was supposed to be. There was one member of the family who counted by millions, and public rumour attributed somewhat equal opulence to the others, and, as these others were very few in number and all rich, the rumour took consistency and the very name became synonymous with 'millionaire'. But so far was I from being the eldest son of a millionaire that I was not an eldest son at all in the sense of being an heir. My father had ten children, and took care to let us all know that he would make no difference between us as to our inheritance: a decision due, in some measure, to his having married a French lady,[1] the beautiful daughter of a distinguished man of science. I was never in any doubt as to my position, nor did it ever cause me the smallest dissatisfaction. But, undoubtedly, I must have arrived at the Rectory with the prestige of being 'the eldest son' of 'a millionaire'. My father's ideas on the subject of inheritance will, however, give only a faint indication of the gulf that separated the world I had come from in London from the world I had come to in the country. Up to this date, no member of the powerful family to which I belonged had so much as thought of seeking an entrance into the class of landed gentry or what is called 'society'. Not one had even attempted to get into Parliament, except a connection by marriage who founded a peerage.[2] All who bore the family name were somewhat eccentric. They did not go to church, and they were not dissenters. They were direct in their ways and very outspoken.

I had been four months in the counting-house when my father surprised me by the welcome intelligence that I was to go to Cambridge. He had yielded to the remonstrances of friends who considered that I had faculties deserving of this cultivation, and, although I did not achieve distinction at the University, I did, indeed, greatly profit by my residence there. I had been always fond of Latin and Greek and mathematics, and had been to a good school, but the exact methods of Cambridge came upon me like a revelation, and the training I there received in classics and mathematics, and which commenced at the Rectory, has been the blessing of my life. I am suspicious of these new Triposes. Between school and the counting-house I had spent a year on the Continent, partly at Dresden (where I learnt German), partly travelling with a friend of my father's over a great part of Europe, the journey ending at Florence. I had been much in France with my kind relations, and knew the language well. And I was a good dancer, of small stature, exactly 5ft. 5in., but of great strength and activity, although somewhat feminine in appearance. I could jump as high as my chin. I was very short-sighted, owing to much reading by a bad light at school, and wore spectacles. I did not smoke. I had no wish to do so, and a great fear that the habit might make me objectionable to ladies, a fear which, in 1838, was not without foundation.

Flintham Church and Vicarage showing the pupil's wing

My tutor was middle-aged, with a young wife[3] and a first baby. He had been a Fellow of a great College at Cambridge, to which his living belonged. It was not in the gift of the family at the Hall, and with them he had no connection; but, being the clergyman of the parish, he received from them that respect which was due to his position.

The Hall was occupied by a widow lady with seven children. The eldest son and heir, about a year older than myself, was at Oxford, and three other boys were at school, one of them at Eton. The three daughters were at home, one about my own age, one rather more than a year younger, and one about 13. There was a governess; and a maiden aunt, who had a house of her own at the market town some six miles distant and was a very frequent visitor.

I first saw these ladies in church. The church was fairly spacious and on opposite sides were two ample well-enclosed pews, the larger belonging to the Hall, the smaller to the Rectory. You could not see from one to the other when sitting, and matters were so arranged that, when standing, you were back to back. But, in spite of these difficulties, I saw enough to make me wish to see more.

My tutor explained to me that I must not expect to make the acquaintance of the young ladies until their brothers came home for the summer holidays, and so matters stood when the day for Queen Victoria's Coronation arrived, and preparations had to be made for a loyal festivity in which the Hall was bound to take a leading part.

Various modes of diversion were provided for the villagers, but the one to which I looked forward was the dance on the green. My tutor had informed me that the young ladies would only be allowed one dance each, and only with himself. But then it would be a country dance! It was a glorious day and in the bright afternoon all the villagers assembled in the spacious enclosure behind the Hall, and the lady of the Hall, with her children and attendants, came out to meet them.

I have called this enclosure the stableyard, but a more correct description is necessary in order that the scene may be realised. The stables occupied only a small part of one side in a line with the churchyard wall, but beyond it. The opposite side opened into garden, park, and shrubberies. One end was covered by one side of the Hall, which was very long, and this side had, in the middle an entrance door (not the main entrance) of some pretensions, with wide stone steps on which stood the Hall party. At the opposite end was a wood with a private road going through it.

The enclosure was half surrounded by trees. A country dance being speedily arranged, the band struck up, the clergyman of the parish leading off with the eldest daughter of the house, and afterwards dancing with each of the other young ladies in succession. In turns each came to me, and though not a word was said, the close approach necessitated by the nature of the dance gave an opportunity for mutual observation which was not lost on either side. I cannot have studied the young ladies more closely than they studied me. What they thought, I had, at the time, no means of knowing. They all attracted me, but more specially the second in age—*'Bessy'*—the name by which she was usually mentioned and by which I have never ceased to think of her from that day to this.

The dance continued, and I continued to dance long after the Hall party had retired. The day ended with a few fireworks and a good deal of noise; but at length the village became quiet, some stars came out and I returned to the Rectory to dream of 'a silver shape'.

CHAPTER II

The Family at the Hall

'THERE ARE SOME TRAITS about the squire's family which appear to me to be national. It is one of those old aristocratical families which are, I believe, peculiar to England, and scarcely understood in other countries; that is to say, families of the ancient gentry, who, though destitute of titled rank, maintain a high ancestral pride; who look down upon all nobility of recent creation, and would consider it a sacrifice of dignity to merge the venerable name of their house in a modern title. This feeling is very much fostered by the importance which they enjoy on their hereditary domains'.

WASHINGTON IRVING

This extract from *Bracebridge Hall* represents better than anything I could say the precise position of the family with which my acquaintance had now commenced. Of the lady of the Hall my tutor and his wife used to speak with respect bordering upon awe. They used to say that 'everyone was afraid of her'. This is a feeling which, no doubt, existed, but which I was never quite able to understand. To me she appeared simply as the most perfect type of good breeding I had ever seen, and now, at the end of a long life, I cannot say that, in this respect, I have ever met her equal. She had not more kindness and consideration for others than I have known other ladies to possess, nor more dignity, but she combined these qualities to a truly remarkable extent. The consequence was that the Hall was a school for good manners. Perhaps some did not like going to this school; I did.

This lady had been the last representative of a family that came to England with the Conquest, and had inherited all their estates. She gave her hand to a distant cousin,[1] who changed his name in order that the name with which the estates were connected might be preserved, and who was described to me as possessing the most stately person and most genial disposition. He had high rank in the army, from which he retired on his marriage. The cause of his early death I did not learn, but I did hear of the love and affection of which he was the object, not only in the domestic circle but in all the wider circles of human life. There was, inevitably, a shade of sadness over his widow, but she showed no tinge of asperity. She was small in person, but perfectly well proportioned and retained her youthful figure. She had dark hair, just beginning to turn grey, and blue eyes. Her eldest daughter could only be described as a youthful reproduction of herself.

'Bessy' was of a different type, and appears to have taken after her father. She was slightly taller than her sister, but not more than 5ft. 3in. She was fuller in outline, but still more graceful. Her complexion was not white and red, like her sister's, but a soft combination of the two colours, somewhat brightened in the cheeks, but diffused all over her neck and arms, and heightened again in her finger tips. I already knew my Homer in those days and she used to recall to me the poet's 'rosy-fingered morn'. Her hair was yellowish and abundant, and hung in many ringlets, which, beginning low down, were quite perpendicular. Her eyes were of a soft light blue, large and beautiful. The only want of perfection that could be detected in her features was a slight projection of the upper teeth, and yet this peculiarity seemed rather to add to than to take away from the sweetness of the mouth. But her great charm was what the Germans call *anmuth*, a geniality which, combined with an overflowing fullness of life, made her irresistible. I did not, in these days, know the second part of *Faust*, but there, in Chiron's description of Helen, are lines which accurately describe this English girl. She was not at all like Washington Irving's Julia in *Bracebridge Hall*. She was not given to blushing. She never seemed to think she had cause to blush. She could glow with pleasure and grow pale with grief, but never attempted to hide her emotions.

The little one was a charming child, something between her two sisters in appearance. She had stronger features than 'Bessy', but the same complexion, rather brighter hair, which she wore in plaits, and eyes not so large but of a deeper blue. She had the wistfulness which belonged to her age. I always had, and still have, a peculiar tenderness for little girls, and this one had no reason to complain of my want of attention.

The eldest son I did not see until the Easter of the following year; but as I am now giving a sketch of the whole family, I may as well say at once that he excited my utmost admiration. He was very tall, 6ft. 2in., perfectly proportioned, with regular features, and his mother's dark hair and blue eyes; but all these advantages of person were as nothing compared with his bearing. In after years he became member for the county, and I once saw him walking in the lobby of the House, but not looking as if he belonged to 'the House'. He was a silent member except on one occasion. He was obliged to speak in order to give the lie to a falsehood which affected his honour, and this he did in ten minutes without one superfluous word, with perfect felicity of expression, and with so much dignity that when, next day, *The Times*, in commenting upon this incident in a short special article, spoke of him as 'a chivalrous gentleman', the writer said nothing more than was universally felt to be due to the person and the occasion.

Of the three boys[2] who were expected home for the holidays, one was an Etonian, the next in age to 'Bessy', and, I think her favourite brother. At any rate he became my favourite, partly, perhaps, because he was so like her. He was destined for the church, a profession for which he did not appear to me to have much vocation; but, then, there was a family living waiting for him. The next boy was the only one of the seven brothers and sisters who did not possess the gift of beauty, but he was a fine manly fellow and was intended for the army. Last came a little fellow with dark hair and rosy cheeks and keen blue eyes who, even at that early age, was recognised as the scholar of the family. There was another living waiting for him.

Of the maiden aunt[3] I must also speak. She was advanced in years and devoted to her nephews and nieces who all loved her; and so did I. And I must give the governess a place in my catalogue. She was a most estimable little lady, and I liked her none the worse because she always kept a sharp eye on me.

It was a month after Coronation Day before the three boys came home, but, in the meantime, things did not stand still. I used to fancy that I received looks of recognition in going out of church. This may have been the effect of my imagination; but near the end of July my tutor and his wife received an invitation to dine at the Hall in which I was included. We were received by the lady and her eldest daughter, and the maiden aunt. Four gentlemen from the neighbourhood made up the party, and, as I then saw the interior of the Hall for the first time, I must now describe it.

The end of the Hall which abutted on to the churchyard looked east. The main entrance was to the west, the stableyard with the village green to the north, and a flower garden to the south. Rectory, Church, and Hall were on a bank some ten feet higher than the lane. We rang the bell at the door which opened into the flower garden at the end of the lane and walked by an inside passage to the main entrance hall at the west. Fronting south were the drawing room, dining room and library in succession opening into one another; all very handsome rooms. The drawing room was very large. It was, in fact, a double room. You entered in the middle and found a complete room on each side. To the right was the fireplace opposite the south windows, at the west end the grand piano and windows, and in the middle the round table. To the left there was scarcely any furniture, so that the space was easily made available for dancing. In this spacious and cheerful room we were received.

The stableyard, Flintham Hall

My tutor presented me, and, the other guests having arrived, we proceeded to the dining room. After dinner, when the ladies had retired, the gentlemen remained together for what I thought a very long time, sipping port wine and discussing county matters, but my tedium was relieved by the presence of a gentleman of whom I had heard and wished very much to see. He was a clergyman and the best rider to hounds in the county;[4] so famous, indeed, was his horsemanship that, if I were, even now, to mention his name, the places and persons I am speaking of would be immediately recognised. I was delighted with him: a slender, gentlemanly man about fifty years of age, with a quiet dark eye and a kindly unpretentious manner that drew me to his side. We shall meet him again.

At length the gentlemen left their seats; we returned to the drawing room for a cup of tea, and there I found an addition to the party. The two younger daughters of the house were present, and, for what remained of the evening, I was in a state of enchantment. I was received with smiles, and, as I have always been notorious for a want of self-restraint in the expression of my feelings by my looks, my admiration for 'Bessy' must have been perceived. Whether there was any music or singing that evening I cannot remember with any certainty. There was not, among these young ladies, any remarkable excellence in this respect. If there had been, I should have remembered it, as I have an ear for music. But no music could have added to my pleasure. How happy I was!

CHAPTER III

Came Glimmering Through the Laurels

DURING THE MONTH OF AUGUST and part of September, the three boys were at home. We were soon good friends, and the Etonian became my constant companion. He often walked with me, and we used to take with us the big black and white Newfoundland, dear old Thetis, who was usually chained up in the stableyard and was very grateful for a run.

It was still difficult to see the young ladies; but, towards the end of the holidays, my tutor and his wife and myself were again invited to dinner, and this time it was a family party, the only other guest being the maiden aunt. On entering the drawing room, I took a seat beside her and made up my mind that she was the lady I ought to take in to dinner. I was ignorant of the rule of etiquette which gives precedence to a married lady, and that I ought to have offered my arm to my tutor's wife, or, at any rate, to have waited for the directions of the lady of the house. So, as soon as dinner was announced, I rose and offered my arm to my neighbour, who hesitated, and instantly came the instruction, 'Mr——[1] will you take Mrs—— in to dinner?' I did not change my attitude, and these words were repeated in a louder tone. But I paid no attention. The lady of the house gave it up, and I led the way to the dining room with the maiden aunt upon my arm in total unconsciousness of the error I had committed.

There was something more in this than ignorance of etiquette. The words addressed to me had reached my ears, but not my understanding. I was drawn very strongly to the most lovable elderly lady who was 'Bessy's' aunt, and a preconceived idea was with me, at that time of life, so all-powerful that I actually was utterly insensible to the meaning of the words I heard so plainly. I had not the slightest intention of offering any slight to my tutor's wife. But she never forgave me.

The eldest daughter and the two elder boys made up the party at table. There was no long sitting over the wine. We were soon all assembled in the drawing room, where the family circle was completed, and, after tea, dancing was proposed. The governess was present and played the piano. We first danced a quadrille and afterwards I waltzed with the three sisters in turn. I have already said that I was a good dancer, and such was the fact. Perhaps my French blood had to do with it. The waltz was my delight, but I never abused its opportunities. I never departed, in the slightest degree, from the respectful demeanour without the observance of which this fascinating dance is liable to become objectionable. Dancing without decorum I could never endure. I loved dancing for its own sake. But one pleasure enhances another when they will combine. The young ladies all danced well, and no consciousness of the mistake I had committed in the early part of the evening interfered to mar my intense enjoyment.

Next morning I found out my mistake, and was sorry for it, but never attempted to explain it; nor do I believe any explanation would have been accepted or have even been understood. It would certainly have appeared to be incredible that the words so plainly addressed to me had not reached my understanding.

This delightful evening, which doubtless I owed to the Etonian, was for me the chief event connected with the

Flintham Hall and Church, 1838

holidays; but although I saw little of the young ladies in my walks with their brother, I then learnt my way about the grounds and the park, and obtained permission to take out Thetis after my young friends had returned to school. My usual time for a walk was about sunset, and I usually began my walk along the footpath which connected the end of the lane with the London road. For a certain distance the high garden wall to the right shut out all view in that direction; but further on came a low hedge over which could be seen at a distance of not much more than a hundred yards, the long raised terrace bordered on both sides by laurels in which were considerable gaps. The fields to the left were meadows divided by rather high banks with hedges on the top. I used to leave the footpath, run along the grass, and Thetis and I together would jump the hedges.

One evening I saw something moving on the terrace and stopped to look. It was a young lady in a white dress, with a straw hat and green veil. I knew the dress, and, although the distance was too great for me to identify the wearer, I could have no doubt as to who it was. It was the dinner hour at the Hall and I knew that only the eldest young lady dined late; and it was not the youngest. The costume was what they all wore out of doors in suitable weather. So there could be no mistake, and, so long as the white dress, straw hat, and green veil remained in view, I did not prolong my walk, but moved about slowly backwards and forwards. At one time the vision that so entranced me would be hidden by the laurels, and would then reappear in the openings. At length it disappeared altogether in the direction of the Hall, and then I resumed my run with Thetis. After this, I never failed to take the same walk daily at the same hour; every now and then were my eyes rejoiced in like manner, and 'Bessy' was sometimes accompanied by her younger sister.

Maud was not published until many years after this date; but I have good reason to believe that one passage in it was already written, the affecting passage containing the line:

Came glimmering through the laurels.

I have, in a scrap book, a copy of this passage which was given to me at Cambridge. The date attached to my copy is January, 1842; but these beautiful verses had long been known in Cambridge. I was allowed to copy them by an intimate friend of Tennyson's, and I remember being told at the same time that that most musical phrase, 'the old Manorial Hall', had already been stolen for the refrain of a new song. The passage in question, which had originally (in a shorter form and with trifling variations) a separate existence from *Maud*, is that which constitutes (in the first edition) the 24th section: a lament appropriate indeed to a tragedy, and not appropriate to my simple tale. 'Bessy' never 'met me'; never did I dream of such a thing; but not the less have I always associated her with the following lines in the lament:

Alas for her that met me,
That heard me softly call,
Came glimmering through the laurels
At the quiet evening fall
In the garden by the turrets
Of the old Manorial Hall.

And when I read the whole poem, on its publication in 1855, I immediately pictured to myself Maud as wearing a white dress when she 'came glimmering through the laurels'.

About this time occurred an incident which is so fresh in my memory that, however insignificant it may appear, I must not pass it over. In church, when standing up, I was exactly back to back with 'Bessy', with the width of the church between us. I had become very greedy for a glimpse of her fair face, and I discovered that, if I was quick enough in turning round when the time came to kneel down, I could obtain one. For some weeks this manœuvre was successful; but there was in the Hall pew the base of a large column on the side towards the aisle, and one Sunday I found that 'Bessy' was behind this column instead of being in her accustomed place. This, I felt sure, was the doing of the governess, as indeed it was. After a few weeks, this good lady fell ill and could not come to church for two Sundays, on each of which 'Bessy' was in her old place.

I was 'like blind Orion hungry for the morn'. I never lost a chance of feeding my eyes. I had remarked that the young ladies made periodical calls at the Rectory, and always at a certain hour. The day I could not tell, but never did I miss being in the Rectory garden at the calling hour. They never came without seeing me. They would think it was chance, but it was no such thing.

So matters stood, and I was considering whether I could arrange to spend any part of the Christmas holidays at the Rectory, when I was informed that the whole family were going to Brighton for the winter, according to their usual custom, the reason for this being that there the young ladies could have instruction in the higher branches of education. When the day of departure came, I took the footpath to the London road and saw the travelling carriage go by. This happened at the end of October.

CHAPTER IV

An Interlude

I FELT DESOLATE, but the hunting season then began, and furnished me with some distraction from the now entirely unsatisfied longings of my heart. My tutor kept a horse and rode to hounds, although in a very mild fashion, as my young friends at the Hall had taken the trouble to inform me. I had no horse to ride in any fashion, nor had I the least desire for one. In later life I kept horses and rode to hounds in no mild fashion; but at this time of my life I had such delight in the exercise of my own powers of running and jumping that I would not have said 'thank you' for a horse.

After the age of 25, although I could still run as well as ever, my jump left me; but I can truly say that I never enjoyed the sensation of a big jump on horseback in my hunting days more than I did when I was one of the 'foot people' at the time I am speaking of. A well-bred horse, with his long pasterns, comes down light from a big drop, and I can remember how I used to alight on the tips of my toes as light as a feather. So I attended all the meets within reach and was soon well known in the hunt.

I remember once, when I made my appearance at the cover-side in the afternoon (after the first run was over and when the hounds were about to draw for a second fox), hearing a good-natured voice say, 'Here we are again, spectacles and all'. Of course, when the hounds ran straight away to the open country, I soon lost them, but quite as often they never left the close country between the London road and the river, and, on these days, there were many horsemen who saw no more of them than I did; some not so much, my tutor, for example. The river was deep; I never knew fox or hounds to cross it. It ran for many miles at a distance of about a mile from the London road, and the strip of country between, besides being well wooded, was stiffly enclosed. The river banks on our side were about a hundred feet high, and were cleft into deep hollows here and there by brooks. On the other side of the London road, that is, to the east, the country was open and nearly level, as fine a stretch of hunting country as is to be found in England.

The pack was famous, and so was the Master,[1] a hearty old English squire, some seventy years of age, with a vigorous frame and a sunburnt face. I once found him alone in a deep lane between woods near the river. The fox was lost, and he asked me if I had seen him. I answered 'no', but that a few days ago I had smelt a fox in this lane. 'Smell a fox', he exclaimed; 'by God, I could smell a joint of roast beef, but in all my life I could never smell a fox'. Let me say, in passing, that twice in my hunting days did I find the fox by scent before the hounds. Would that my senses were now equally acute!

When out with the hounds, I often saw and always received a kind greeting from the hard-riding clergyman whose acquaintance I had made at the Hall, and at last it so happened that I had the very great pleasure of being of use to him. He was not satisfied with riding a good horse and going to the front, to enjoy himself thoroughly he required to have a young horse to teach. With such horses his numerous friends were always ready to provide him, so that he may fairly be said to have been horse-breaker to the county. The consequence was numerous falls. He always took his own line, and, one day, I found him alone standing beside his horse, which was lying on its back in a narrow ditch, wedged in so tight that our united efforts to get him out were fruitless. So I ran off to the nearest farmhouse and brought a man with a spade, and then, after a good deal of excavation, the horse was got upon his legs.

'I had no horse to ride'

The hounds helped me over a dreary period, and at Christmas I went home. My father had two houses;[2] one some eight miles north of London, quite in the country, with a few fields attached to it, and a very large garden as beautiful as it was productive; the other was in the immediate neighbourhood of Russell Square. Both houses were large and comfortable. My father had a passion for gardening, and used to live at his country house from the beginning of May until the end of October, driving to London in his carriage three days a week; the winter months he spent in London.

On my arrival, I found a large party assembled, brothers, sisters, and cousins, who gave me a hearty welcome. And yet, in the very welcome, there was to me a jarring note. They seemed to me to be too noisy and a little rough. I had not anticipated that I should feel this, but the effect upon me was instantaneous. My nerves were, no doubt, in a peculiarly sensitive condition, but there was a deeper cause than this for what I felt. I had been at school at the Hall as well as at the Rectory, and had brought back with me not only a good deal of Greek and Algebra, but also a different standard of social observances, even of children towards one another. I had acquired a new sense and had undergone a change in myself which marked an epoch in my life, and although this happened in connection with my first introduction into what is called 'county society', it must not be supposed that the position of the 'family at the Hall' had, in itself, any influence upon me whatever. But they had, one and all, a surpassing charm of manner to which my inner nature responded.

A few years later I found a similar charm in the family of a Birmingham manufacturer; the distinction between town and county has nothing to do with what I am saying. It is quite true that, in 1838, that distinction was much more strongly marked than at present, and I had become fully aware of it, but that did not trouble me.

Troubled I was when I got home by an immediate perception of the difficulties there would be in bringing my own family into agreeable communication with the family into which I hoped to enter. Not that there was anything serious to complain of, but my beautiful and most loving mother spoilt all her children, and was allowed to do so. She spoilt me, and that she had done so I, at this time, discovered. After I had been to school at the Hall, I began to look at myself from a point of view which was not my mother's point of view. I became conscious of my own deficiencies.

My mother was no mere petty weak-minded woman. On the contrary, she inherited much of the intellect of her distinguished father and had great practical ability. But, in her, the feelings of maternity were overpowering to a degree to which I have never seen a parallel. She lived to a great age, surrounded by children, grand-children, and great-grand-children, and, never to the last lost sight of the fortunes or even the health of any one of them. She never thought that she could have too many descendants and could only with difficulty see a fault in any of them.

My father saved money for all his large family, and was also most liberal to us in his lifetime. He was of a most affectionate disposition, but was occasionally choleric, when he would speak sharply and write as he would have spoken, not reflecting that, while an angry word can be dealt with on the spot and if unjust be shown at once to be so, the same is not the case with a letter. It is a mistake to say that you should write as you would speak. More care is required, because a mistake is not so easily corrected. My father himself used to quote the Latin proverb, 'littera scripta manet', but he sometimes forgot it. He disliked society and would seldom go to other people's houses, but kept open house himself. Every day a few spare covers were laid at table, and it very rarely happened that no one arrived to partake of the good fare that was every day provided, and of the old port of which my father had enough to set up many a wine merchant. Not that wine merchants keep their port wine so long as he did. But he was very temperate. He had seen hard drinking days in his youth, when hard drinking was a national custom, but a change for the better was pretty well established in 1838, and nowhere more decidedly than at his hospitable table.

It was a cheerful, happy home I came to. And yet my enjoyment was clouded over by a certain sense of incongruity between the ways of my own people and those of my new friends. I was not disturbed because we lived near Russell Square. Most heartily did I agree with my father, when, in somewhat profane language, he used to denounce the folly of many of our neighbours who, at that date, were moving westward to houses at double the rent and with half the accommodation. He used to tell a good story on this subject.

He declared that one M.P. having mentioned Russell Square in the House of Commons, another M.P., 'an impudent coxcomb', as my father used to call him, thereupon enquired 'if the honourable gentleman could inform him where Russell Square was' and that immediately the rents went down one half.

No, it was nothing of this sort that troubled me. This is a point I would gladly have passed over, but I am writing my confessions, and truth obliges me to say that in the family at the Hall I had found a high refinement of manner to which I had not been accustomed. About this there was nothing artificial. It seemed to me to be, and I am sure it was, 'an outward and visible sign of an inward and spiritual grace'.

Before I quit this topic, I may as well say that I do not think that the enormous popularity of the writings of Charles Dickens, when they first appeared, had a happy influence upon manners. The present generation can have no idea of the rage for Dickens at the time of this narrative. Like all the rest, I was much amused; but, at last, I was literally persecuted by 'Sam Wellerisms', which I was expected to take for conversation as well as wit. I can enjoy my Dickens now, but am glad not to hear so much of it.

There was a shadow over me, as has been seen; but, all the same, I spent a merry Christmas at Russell Square among brothers, sisters, and cousins, and, in the first days of February, 1839, I returned to the Rectory.

CHAPTER V

The Old Pocket Book

So FAR I HAVE HAD nothing but my memory to guide me in my narrative; but my memory is very good, and I am confident that it has not misled me. Moreover, we all know how much the accuracy of our recollection of events depends upon the impression they make upon us at the time that they occur.

There are circumstances and persons that pass by us and leave not a trace behind, others that engrave themselves upon our very being. Using the word 'love' in its widest significance, it may be truly said that memory is the child of love; and thus do I explain to myself the truly extraordinary faculty which I possessed in my youth of remembering certain things I read.

At the very good school[1] I went to from the age of ten to the age of fifteen, learning by heart did not enter into the system of instruction, and yet, after reading the first four books of the *Aeneid*, I found that I knew them by heart, and delighted with the discovery actually did repeat them, with scarcely a single fault, to a schoolfellow: one who afterwards distinguished himself in the public service and met with a tragic end in Abyssinia.[2]

The few Greek plays which I studied with care I could say by heart. Now, was this owing to any mere faculty of recollection? Was it not mainly due to the intensity of my admiration for the verses of Virgil and the Greek dramatists?

And what is poetry in words to poetry in persons? If we are so much affected in reading about Helen or Antigone, what should we feel if we actually met them? I can remember well putting to myself a question of this description in my Cambridge days, and coming to the conclusion that the personal charm of the magic of which I had had experience during the period of my relations with the family at the Hall was something 'better than all treasures that in books are found'. No, my memory has not misled me!

Nevertheless, I am not sorry now to have the assistance of some memoranda in an old pocket book,[3] a *Peacock's Pocket Journal* for 1839, in which I began to keep a diary from the date of my return to the Rectory. The memoranda are very brief, and mostly in German and in the German written character; not intelligible to anyone but myself, and to me of value chiefly because they give the precise dates of unforgotten days. There is no diary for January, but the space is not blank. Here I find some unsuccessful attempts to express my feelings in verse; among them an acrostic. I had not then read Addison's papers in the *Spectator* on 'False Wit', or I should not have attempted this form of composition; but the acrostic is not worse than the rest, and there is in it one line which I see reason to give:

Hold thee I may not, phantom of a dream,

for, although not written with any intentional reference to my dreams at this period, not the less does it very truly give their general character.

I have always been a great dreamer, and have, indeed, in the course of my life, had some very remarkable dreams. I have seen the future in a dream, I have received warnings in dreams, unfortunately not attended to. I once saw a place in a dream years before I saw it with my bodily eyes; I even once had a dream-meeting of somewhat the same sort as those described by Du Maurier in *Peter Ibbetson*. My dreams have always been to me an important part of my life; but at no time of my life did they so persistently run in one channel as they did at the time I am speaking of.

For months together it was the rarest thing for me to shut my eyes in sleep without immediately seeing the object of my daily thoughts, and one particular dream was of constant recurrence. I used to fancy myself floating in the air somewhere in the neighbourhood of the Hall, then I would see 'Bessy' walking beneath me, then I would stoop to seize her, the wind of my approach would seem to drive her just out of my reach, and then I would wake. Night after night did this dream pursue me, and was most frequent at the time of my return to the Rectory.

The old pocket book tells me that I slept at the market town[4] on Saturday, February 2nd, 1839. On Sunday morning I went to church there, my object being to see the kind aunt. I went to her pew and then to her house, and learnt from her that the family had not yet returned from Brighton. I then walked the six miles to the Rectory, arriving in time for afternoon service; how sad to me was that afternoon service is duly noted in my diary.

On Thursday, the 7th, part of the family returned; on Friday I had a hard run with the hounds; and on Saturday the rest of the family returned, 'to my great joy', as duly noted in the old pocket book. The entry for Sunday I give under reserve; it may have been due to an illusion. It simply states in German that '"Bessy" pressed my hand'. I can remember well speaking to the whole party as we came out of church and that all seemed glad to see me and gave me their hands, and that I certainly pressed 'Bessy's' hand, and returned to the Rectory in great delight, believing that the pressure had been returned, very slightly indeed, but still, as I fancied, distinctly; and I can also remember the long consideration I gave to this circumstance before I decided on making a note of it.

On Wednesday, the 13th, I met the governess out walking

with 'Bessy' and her younger sister, and on Friday, the 15th, with all three. On such occasions there would be just a few words, but there would also be a giving of hands, and to me these meetings were important events. On Sunday, the 17th, 'a look from "Bessy" ' is the event of the morning service, and in the afternoon in going out of church I contrived to have a word with all three, and to take 'Bessy's' hand. On Thursday, the 21st, I had a run with the hounds. On Sunday, 24th, I contrived to exchange a distant salutation with the three young ladies after the morning service, but was not able to get near them in the afternoon. That same Sunday I took a walk to the river, and of the river I must now speak.

I was fond of fishing and sometimes used to fish there, to very little purpose. Later in life I became a skilful angler, but in these days I was a mere beginner, and had never once yet attempted to throw a fly. The river was not a trout stream, and was full of coarse fish, but was said to hold some large grayling. All the fish I caught this spring are duly entered in the old pocket book, but the catches are so insignificant that I shall not record them afresh, and although it is necessary to mention my fishing, it was not the love of sport that chiefly made the riverside my favourite resort.

The river itself was the attraction. Up to the market town it was navigable; but in our part of the country, although still a considerable stream, its industrial functions were confined to turning mills, and here and there were weirs obstructing the channel. One of those weirs was just about a mile and a half from the Rectory, and this was the point on the river to which I usually bent my steps. There was a deep still pool above the weir, and lively streams below it. The mill was opposite, in a wide expanse of level country. On our side was a narrow stretch of grass, backed by a steep hillside, which rose to about a hundred feet above the water, and was thickly wooded except in the immediate neighbourhood of the pool above the weir, where the trees had been recently cut down.

The weir

This spot was my favourite resort, sometimes for fishing, more often for meditation upon the perfections of 'Bessy'. It was approached by a lane which ran from the London road, in continuation of the lane that connected the London road with the village, and also by a footpath which ran from the London road in continuation of the footpath from the village which joined the London road, this being the footpath already mentioned as passing below the Hall and commanding a view of the terrace. The footpath and the lane were about half a mile apart at the points at which they joined the London road. Then they converged, but the footpath stopped at a cottage inhabited by an old servant of the family, good old Nanny Thorpe.[5] She had been nurse to all the children, and they used often to go and see her, and so did I. But to get from her cottage to the weir a little jumping was necessary. This was no impediment to me, and so the footpath was my usual route to the weir.

All the past summer, sometimes with my useless fishing rod, sometimes without it, had I frequented this lovely spot. I do not think that there is any charm in nature quite equal to the charm of running water.[6] On this visit the river was in flood and not looking its best; the sun was not shining, and the trees, of course, not yet in leaf. But I went again next day and caught a few fish, and from this time forward I resumed my walks to the fields above the weir, not forgetting to look in upon Nanny Thorpe. It was delightful to me to hear her talk about the young ladies, and it will be seen by the sequel that I was able, in the end, to be of some service to her.

And now I must once more refer to *Bracebridge Hall.* There is a chapter called 'Family Servants', beginning as follows:

'In my casual anecdotes of the Hall, I may often be tempted to dwell on circumstances of a trite and ordinary character. It seems to be the study of the squire to adhere, as much as possible, to what he considers the old landmarks of British manners. His servants all understand his ways, and, for the most part, have been accustomed to them from infancy; so that, upon the whole, the household presents one of the few tolerable specimens that can be met with of the establishment of an English country gentleman of the old school'.

Washington Irving then goes on to give a very amusing description of the housekeeper, and although this description will by no means apply to the housekeeper at the Hall we are now concerned with, she also, like Nanny Thorpe, was an old and highly respected servant and the whole establishment resembled very closely that of *Bracebridge Hall.* And somehow I found out that 'Miss Bessy' was the idol of the household.

CHAPTER VI

The Rectory

ON FRIDAY, March 1st, my tutor, his wife, and myself attended a dinner party, at the Hall. It was a formal party and my friend, the clergyman horse-breaker, was not present. I found it tiresome; and, strange to say, after having looked forward, most eagerly, to seeing 'Bessy' in the drawing room after dinner, when I did see her, I was disappointed, and returned to the Rectory in very low spirits. Next day the good aunt called with the three young ladies, and, of course, found me in the garden; but the interview did me no good, and, on the Sunday, I made no attempt at communication with 'Bessy'. I did not look her way either in church or in coming out. I took a walk to the river, my usual resource when in low spirits, but without obtaining relief. What was the matter?

I had, at this time two causes for distress, one that I had begun to doubt the depth of my love, the other that I had come to dislike my tutor. The doubt did not last long, and I cannot account for its origin. Such experiences are, I believe, not unusual, in the growth of the strongest affections. Coventry Patmore, the poet of the love that Swedenborg, with fine euphony, terms 'conjugial love', takes this view of the case, and when I came to read *The Angel in the House* some years later than the time I am speaking of, I at once recognised, in his description, the phase of self-doubt in the progress of my passion which I was now passing through. But it seemed to me at the time that I was ceasing to care for 'Bessy', and this unhappy feeling coinciding with the growth of my aversion to my tutor, resulted in something very like despair.

I remember well, during one of my solitary walks, putting to myself the question whether I had not better ask my father to remove me from the Rectory, and it seemed to me that, from every point of view, this would be right; but I had no strength to take that step. My reason approved of it, but I could not tear myself away, and this was the end of my doubt. I did, however, determine to remove all misconceptions that might exist at the Hall as to my true position, and with this object in view I did on the following Sunday, March 10, pay a visit to my good friend the aunt at her house in the market town.

I went to church there in the morning, took lunch with the dear lady, and afterwards sat with her so long that I was too late for afternoon service at the Rectory. I told her all about the ten children and the equal division of inheritance. I even mentioned the amount there would be to divide, which, as it turned out, I greatly underestimated, and ended by saying that I was intended for the bar and determined to do my best to succeed.

'Then you will have to work', said the lady sympathetically.

'Yes', I replied.

I came to another determination at this time, which I scrupulously adhered to, but this was of a negative description. I decided not to attempt to involve 'Bessy' in any formal engagement. To do this would, I felt sure, bring trouble, and be a poor return to her mother for all her kindness. I was beginning now to feel sure of myself, but I felt that to propose to bind the young lady whilst she was still in the schoolroom and I was preparing for Cambridge would, under the circumstances, be wrong. If I had really been 'the eldest son (and heir) of a millionaire', I should not have hesitated, but my position being what it was, I felt that only an affection which would endure without a tie for some few years at least could by any possibility overcome all the difficulties of the case. That my own affection would be lasting I could no longer doubt. It was the pain of parting from 'Bessy' that alone prevented me, at this time, from leaving my tutor. My position at the Rectory had become nearly unbearable, and how this had come about I must now explain.

My tutor was equally good in classics and mathematics, and taught me so well that I am reluctant to speak of him otherwise than with gratitude; but he had a personal peculiarity that made living with him disagreeable. He was parsimonious in a manner that gave me continual offence. I say 'in a manner', not 'in a degree'. I have known other men more parsimonious, but never one who so much excited others against himself by parsimonious ways as did my tutor. I shall abstain from giving any particulars, but, although his sermons were good, he had no influence in the village, and this was the reason. And the feeling at the Hall was the same as in the village. The lady at the head of the family was indeed most scrupulous in the observance of all social obligations towards the Rectory; but, nevertheless, her sons, being of a peculiarly open hearted and generous disposition, did not disguise their animosity from me.

I was, for a long time, quite happy with my tutor. During the past summer we had spent a fortnight together taking a walking tour in North Wales, and he had taken me with him when he paid a visit to his widowed mother, who lived some twenty miles away in a picturesque old town in the neighbourhood of one of the 'stately homes of England' which he wished me to see. He was a self-made man. The fellowships at our universities are the rewards of scholarship. He must have had a hard struggle in his youth, and that he should then have contracted and have afterwards retained parsimonious habits was only natural. But these habits were not, in themselves, the cause of my annoyance. My comfort was never interfered with.

The mischief was that my tutor had a way of expressing himself about matters of domestic economy which savoured of insult to those whom he addressed, and that, on several occasions since my return after the Christmas holidays, I had felt myself to be insulted by him.

There is an entry in the old pocket book saying that he had 'insulted me at table', and this reminds me of a speech he once made to his wife at table in my presence. The dinner had not been well cooked, indeed very badly; but I felt for the lady when he told her, with the flush of anger on his face, that 'dinner was the only thing worth living for in the country'. I exchanged looks with my tutor's wife, but I am afraid that was the only time we were ever in complete sympathy.

I subsequently added another offence to that of my behaviour at the dinner party at the Hall. My tutor's wife came from a distant county, and, one afternoon, gave me a full account of her family, and did all she could to impress upon me their importance. I listened unmoved, and she finally became excited and turned red in the face. She no doubt thought me incredulous; the truth was that I was simply indifferent.

I have, all my life, been indifferent as to who people were or who were their ancestors, except in connection with transmitted qualities or remarkable achievements, and as, in this case, there were no such circumstances to move my interest, I could feel none, and, I am afraid, allowed this to appear more plainly than was polite. And this was not all. I had never liked the excessive consideration which this lady gave to mere birth and rank. We were as far asunder as the poles on this point, and she must have felt our antagonism as I did. The unfortunate conversation about her own family occurred some little time after my unlucky refusal to take her in to dinner, and it seems to me not unlikely that she wanted me to know that she was a person of more importance than I supposed.

I did not see the danger; I was not in this month of March troubled about my tutor's wife, but solely about himself.

He had 'got upon my nerves' as the saying is, and, for the only time in my life, I began to feel hate. I am very sensitive to anything in the nature of an insult, and, without in the least intending it, he had roused up in me such a feeling that I felt it was becoming wrong for me to live any longer with him.

Flintham Vicarage, main front

I remember once, at this time, walking behind him with an impulse of hatred in my heart which terrified me. I have always, since this experience, felt the greatest compassion for people who are under the obligation to live together, but between whom has arisen an aversion which the mere presence of each must continue to aggravate in the other. I have said that 'memory is the child of love', but it may also be said that 'memory is the child of hate'. I remember nothing better than the unhappy days when I was under the influence of this emotion; but I should never have given them a place in this record were it not necessary for the explanation of subsequent events, and to make it clear that when I now decided to stay at the Rectory I was under the sway of a more powerful emotion of an opposite character.

I subdued my angry feeling, which, in spite of all that happened afterwards, never again returned in equal force, and on Sunday, the 17th, after two weeks, during which I had neither seen nor attempted to see 'Bessy', we met again with joy on my part and smiles on hers. Her mother was not in church, and the governess could not prevent a short conversation between me and her three charges after we came out. And on Wednesday, the 20th, the three boys came home for the Easter holidays.

CHAPTER VII

The Easter Holidays

FOR THREE WEEKS was I all abandoned to delight. The morning after his arrival the Etonian came to see me, much grown and altered, and, as the hounds would be within reach the next day, Friday, March 22, we agreed to go out on foot together. The Etonian was now about as tall as I was, and a fine handsome cheery young fellow. This day the hounds ran clean away to the open country; but we persevered and came up with them at a check, then we lost them again, but still we followed the line, and when, at last, we were obliged to give in, we found that we were ten miles from home. Then, after a glass of the famous ale of the county (a glass of ale which I well remember) we trotted back. Next day, Saturday, the hounds met at the Hall; foxes were plentiful, but the hounds never got far away, and we kept up with them all day without trouble.

Sunday, the 24th, I saw a good deal of 'Bessy'. Again her mother was not in church, and, after the service, the young ladies introduced me to their eldest brother, who had now arrived from Oxford. In the afternoon he called at the Rectory with his two elder sisters. I was, as usual, in the garden, and walked back with them to the Hall. There I saw the youngest of the sisters, who had not been at church in the morning, not being at this time quite so well as usual; but I have a memorandum saying she was 'looking beautiful'. Like the

Etonian, she was now growing fast. To me she was never anything but a child, but I took great delight in her.

I also met the Etonian and the brother next to him. We agreed to go fishing together, and I showed them my fishing tackle and they showed me theirs. Moreover, I became very friendly with the eldest son. On the Monday I went fishing with the two boys, and caught a few fish, but they caught nothing. A violent storm came on, and we got very wet and dirty, but we collected sticks and lighted a fire and finally made our way to a little riverside inn, where we obtained shelter and refreshment, after which we returned all very happy at the close of a long and somewhat trashing day. On the Tuesday afternoon the Etonian came for me, and I went with him to the Hall to help him and his brother to garden. The gardening consisted of spade work among the laurels, where some alterations had to be made. I saw only the youngest sister, who was now out again, but I was in high spirits. On the Wednesday I was over at the Hall and hard at work before breakfast, and again before the early dinner at the Rectory: on my way back I saw 'Bessy' at a window, and she 'nodded to me and smiled at me' as I duly recorded. Again in the evening I assisted in some ferreting, the eldest son being of the party.

So, there were three visits in one day, but they were all short, and did not interfere with my studies. That same day I worked at Greek for five hours, and for two hours at trigonometry. My diary tells me this. I kept as careful an account of my studies as I did of every incident connected with my love. But, on the Thursday, I had but just worked for an hour and a half when the Etonian arrived with an invitation which put an end to my studies for that day—and for the next. He asked me to spend the day with himself and his brothers ferreting, and I left my books and went away with him. We went with the good old keeper to a distant part of the estate, and when we returned to the Hall it was late, and I was asked to join the family at dinner.

This unexpected invitation threw me into a transport of joy. I rushed off to my bedroom at the Rectory and was back at the Hall in evening dress within ten minutes from the time of receiving the invitation; much earlier than necessary; I knew that there was no occasion for hurry but I was in an ecstasy of impatience. I was the only guest. 'Bessy' did not appear at dinner, but came in to dessert with her younger sister and the youngest boy, and took a seat opposite to me. What a beautiful sight was that dinner table with the good lady at the head of it and all her seven children about her. How favoured I was! And I could not help remarking how polite they all were to one another at table.

We young men did not sit long over our wine, but soon followed the ladies to the drawing room, and then, after a little singing, of which I remember nothing, came waltzing, which I can never forget, and then a game at cards which I enjoyed even more than the waltzing. We eight sat down at the round table, and I secured a seat near 'Bessy'. The game was one that turns upon the cards being all pairs, there being an odd card in the pack which cannot be paired. It is a game for young unmarried people. If, at the end of the game, a gentleman is left with the odd card, he is proclaimed 'Old Bachelor'; if a young lady, she is proclaimed 'Old Maid'. We played two games, and I was made Old Bachelor and 'Bessy' Old Maid amid shouts of laughter.

It did not occur to me at the time that the others were cheating, but it occurs to me now, and a little reflection makes me sure of this. I had never seen this amusing game before, but I have played at it since, and have myself cheated. The fun of the game greatly depends upon the odd card being left with the right person, and to make me Old Bachelor and 'Bessy' Old Maid whilst we were sitting side by side was doubly diverting.

She looked ravishing this evening. Evening dress always became her, but this was the occasion when she recalled to me

Homer's favourite epithet for Eos. She wore black mittens, from which emerged the slender rosy fingers, and I must confess that I contrived once or twice to touch the tips of her fingers with the tips of mine as we were pushing the cards about. The next day 'I could do nothing but think of her and write nonsense'.

On Saturday, the 30th, a gentleman called[1] at the Rectory, and made my acquaintance, of whom I must give some account. He was an uncle of my young friends, a resident fellow of a college at Cambridge, about fifty years of age, tall, straight, and still handsome. I had a long conversation with him. He told me that in his youth he had been just as fond of waltzing as I was now, and a great jumper. I found out that he was an accomplished fly-fisher, and I asked him to give me a lesson in this beautiful art which he promised to do if there was a favourable opportunity. I was charmed with him. This afternoon I was at a garden party at the Hall, that is, I worked hard among the laurels with the boys and 'Bessy' and her younger sister, who both worked as hard as any of us. This was, in truth, a fine illustration of what Fourier calls 'attractive industry'. What industrial wonders might not be accomplished by such combinations! This evening the eldest brother lent me the last number of *Nicholas Nickleby*.

On Sunday, March 31st, I took a walk with the Etonian, and we went to the stables to see a fox with nine cubs in honourable captivity. His two younger sisters were with us at the stables, and my diary says that ' "Bessy" was looking beautiful'.

Monday, April 1st, was bright and frosty, and the morning indeed was so cold that, had I not been such a complete novice in the gentle art, I could hardly have been taken in by the note which I received from the eldest brother, saying that 'his uncle desired him to tell me that if I would meet him at the weir at ten he would give me a lesson in fly-fishing'; and it was not until I had been at the weir for two hours that it suddenly occurred to me that this was the 1st of April. Then away I ran to the Hall to join in the laugh against myself, only too glad to have an excuse for a call; and, indeed, I had much the best of the joke, for I met 'Bessy' alone in the garden. My diary records my embarrassment and my inability 'to say any of the tender things I had prepared for such an occasion', and speaks of 'innocent looks by which I was disarmed'. I fancy I can see her now standing among the laurels.

Tuesday, April 2nd, is a red letter day in this short calendar of happiness. I met the Etonian, and he asked me to spend the evening with them under the following circumstances: his mother with the eldest brother and sister were going to a county ball at a great distance and would not be at home. So I joined the remainder of the party, who were under the charge of the uncle and the governess.

The first entertainment was snap-dragon, the preparations for which were made in the library. When all was ready, we went in and the lights were put out as soon as the bowl of brandy was set on fire. There was great merriment over the snatching of the plums, but the play of the light on 'Bessy's' features was more interesting to me than the plums. Then the candles were lighted again, and the room cleared for blind man's buff.

The table which rested on a pivot in the centre was turned up and pushed to one side, but the legs would not allow it to go quite close to the wall, so that there was a narrow passage with only room for one between the table and the side of the room up to one corner. The end of the table away from the wall was a little dangerous. Before the game began I heard the governess tell the little boy to keep between me and his sister, but I took good care that he did no such thing. One of the boys was blind-folded, then another, and eventually I contrived to get caught. My object was of course to catch 'Bessy'. I did not succeed, but my intention was very evident, and my attempts caused much excitement and amusement. I never responded to the touches of the boys, but, whenever I heard 'Bessy's'

Blind Man's Buff

voice I made a dart in that direction. Once I did lay a hand upon her, but she slipped away. I should have caught her at last but for my own stupidity. She had taken refuge in the corner behind the table, and suspecting this, but being afraid of hitting my head against the end of the table, I went down on my hands and knees and crawled between the table and the wall. I was close to her and she could not have escaped, when an unaccountable impulse (which I am inclined to attribute to some adverse spirit) caused me to turn back. A shout of laughter told me of my mistake, and after this I gave it up and caught one of the boys.

We afterwards played at Old Bachelor and Old Maid, and so that evening did I take another 'long draught of love'.

On Wednesday, April 3, I was a good deal with the Etonian, and next day there was a most amusing steeplechase among the village lads, the course having been marked out by the eldest brother. It seemed to me that the line was impossible for there were one or two thorn fences so stiff and so big that I could not conceive of any way of either getting over them or through them. But when the rustics came to them, they jumped and turned round in jumping so that they fell with their backs on the fence and then rolled over into the next field, heels over head. The winner was a lad known by the name of 'Tol'. This day I met 'Bessy' and her little sister in the lane behind the stableyard and stayed with them as long as I could, but they did not come to the steeplechase. On the Friday there was some more industry, but less 'attractive'. Nevertheless, I enjoyed helping the boys to clean out the chicken yard. On the Saturday, I went to the river and paid a visit to Nanny Thorpe, and on Sunday I walked with all the brothers. The three sisters went with us to look at the fox cubs, and when one of the young ladies said they were not pretty one of their brothers answered that 'they were much prettier than *they* were'.

Monday, the 8th, was again a great day. I walked to the market town with the Etonian and the brother next to him. There we took lunch with the kind aunt, then walked the six miles back, and afterwards came an evening under the same conditions as the last, the mother with the eldest son and daughter having gone to another county ball. Again, there was blind man's buff, but the governess would not allow the young ladies to be present, which I did not like at all; and again we played at Old Bachelor and Old Maid. My diary says, ' "Bessy" looked like an angel, came home sad with love', and also records that the little sister told me that ' "Bessy" weighed 8 stone 10 lbs', and that my own weight at this time was 9 stone 11 lbs.

This was the last of the Easter festivities, but the few remaining days before the boys went back to school were to me very eventful. On the Tuesday I met 'Bessy' again alone, and my diary is so audacious as to say, 'loves me, I think, for she squeezed my hand'. The squeezing was probably all on my part.

On the Wednesday I saw no one, but on the Thursday, the 11th, I had a most affectionate parting with the Etonian who was to leave the next day. We took a walk together in the evening and we talked about his sisters. He spoke very warmly of 'Bessy', saying how kind and good-tempered she was, and I joined in her praises with equal warmth. Then he suddenly said, 'Why don't you kiss sister Bess?' My only answer was a grave silence. I was by no means slack, at this time of my life, in taking advantage of opportunities of this description, but I was now under the influence of a feeling such as I had never before experienced—a feeling so intense and so serious and respectful that it prevented me from taking any notice of the boy's imprudent words, and even from making any record of them. My diary merely says that 'I could not tell him how much I loved his sister'; but how could I forget what he had said?

Under my silence was concealed an agitation which comes back upon me even now whilst I write these lines. This parting with the Etonian made me very miserable. He had attached himself to me, and I had become very fond of him for his own sake as well as his sister's sake. We promised to write to one another, and he gave me his address at Eton. The next morning I saw him and his next brother off by the coach, and in the afternoon I took a walk with Thetis.

CHAPTER VIII

The Violets

As I HAVE ALREADY SAID, my little tale is no tragedy, and yet, when the violets[1] come into it, comes so much sorrow mixed up with all the sweetness of my life that I have not thought it inappropriate to present the flower which gives its name to this chapter in its mourning aspect. The violet is the symbol of early death as well as of early love.

Serious trouble with my tutor began even before the happy Easter holidays were quite over. On the morning of Tuesday, April 9th, he came to my room before I was dressed and told me that there was room there for a second bed, and that he was going to write to Cambridge to ask the same friend, who had found me for him, to find him a second pupil. Now my room was comfortable, but not large (how well I remember it with the window looking over the churchyard towards the Hall), and, considering the very handsome sum which my tutor received for his charge of me, I had every right to object to his proposition, and I did so that day as soon as I had recovered from my painful surprise. On this point my diary is explicit. He refused to entertain my objections, and I had to consider what I should do.

There was a very simple remedy. If I had told him that I should not be allowed to remain with a second pupil, he would (as it turned out) have dropped the idea at once; but, above all things, I wished to avoid a collision which might end in a separation. I could not bear the idea of leaving the Rectory sooner than the time fixed for my going to Cambridge, which was in October. But the very reasons which made me so anxious to stay out my full time at the Rectory were the cause of my violent dislike to the coming of a second pupil.

I am not in the least of a jealous disposition, and no feeling of that kind influenced me. But in the course of the Easter holidays I had become intimate with the family at the Hall, and I feared the embarrassment that might be caused by the presence of another youth whom possibly they might not like, although, at the same time, they might not think it right to make too marked a difference between him and me. I refer, of course, to the line of conduct that the head of the family might think it proper to pursue under the circumstances.

My fears were not illusory. There had been a pupil before me at the Rectory, and he had not been liked at the Hall. So I brooded over the situation until at last I took a fatal resolution. Cambridge was only half a day's journey off by coach, and I had a friend there who had asked me to spend a few days with him. I determined to go. I knew the College Don to whom my tutor had written. I proposed to myself to find out if there was any chance of a second pupil coming, and, perhaps, to give a hint of my feelings on the subject. This was not straightforward; the very idea was wrong, and its execution brought about the very catastrophe which I was striving to prevent.

In the meantime the violets made their appearance. I saw the first on this very 9th of April, the same day on which, as mentioned in the last chapter, I pressed 'Bessy's' hand and supposed that she had pressed mine in return. The violets were growing in the clearing of the riverside woods on the steep bank just below Nanny Thorpe's cottage, and above the narrow grass field where was the weir. The clearing was about two acres in extent. At first the violets were scarce, but they increased in number day by day, blue, lilac, and white, all strongly scented, until the whole clearing was covered. Among them were occasional forget-me-nots, and never in all my life have I seen such another bed of violets. It was in full bloom a week after I first discovered it, and, in the meantime, my life did not stand still.

On Sunday, the 14th, I went with 'Bessy's' eldest brother to see the fox cubs, but could not manage to speak to herself, although, as my diary says, 'she smiled on me as usual in coming out of church'. Precious smiles. Little did I know how precious when I made this entry!

On Monday, the 15th, I went to the Hall to play with the little boy who had not yet gone back to school, and my diary speaks of 'a bow and arrow and a squirt'. Anything to be near 'Bessy'. I saw her and her two sisters in the garden, and they introduced me to two cousins who had just arrived; one a slim growing girl of about thirteen, the other a round little thing between nine and ten, both exceedingly lovely, but in quite a different style from the three sisters. They had both dark hair and dark eyes with pale but healthy complexions. The elder was grave and pensive, the little one arch and full of fun, and *her* name was 'Bessy'. So now there were *two* 'Bessies', and it was easy to see that they clung together. I remember being somewhat bewildered when I saw these five young ladies all together, but my diary merely says of this occasion that ' "Bessy" looked very interesting'.

On Tuesday, the 16th, I gathered a great number of violets and called with them at the Hall. I explained where I had found them, and the young ladies said they would go and get some themselves. On Wednesday I brought back an immense quantity in a large basket. I was two hours picking them. I was afraid to call again, and walked about in the churchyard with the basket for a long time in a state of intense agitation. I was still uncertain what to do when I saw the house-keeper's friendly face at her open window which looked into the churchyard. Then I took heart and handed up to her the basket of violets, with a request that she would give it to the ladies with my compliments, and this she undertook to do. Thursday was uneventful, on Friday I took a walk with Thetis, and on Saturday, the 20th, I went to Cambridge.

When there I saw the College Don my tutor had written to. He asked me if I was content with my life at the Rectory, and I said I was. He then said my tutor had written to him asking him to get another pupil for him, but that he saw little chance of finding one. I said I was glad to hear this, and he rejoined, 'You need not be afraid'.

On Wednesday, the 24th, I returned to the Rectory and there found a letter from my father ordering me not to sleep there a single night with anyone in my room. I had written to my father at the same time that I went to Cambridge, and this letter might even now have saved everything had it been written in more gentle terms. He was justly indignant that, considering what he paid, I should not be allowed to have my room to myself; but his letter was so sharp that I was afraid to show it.

On Thursday that week I met the two 'Bessies' in the park, and we were some time together, but my diary says that both on this day and the next I was unhappy and too much agitated to read, 'thinking of all that has happened so lately'. On Saturday my tutor annoyed me by something he said, and I caught some fish and gave them to Nanny Thorpe. And now I come to two memorable days.

On Sunday, April 28, as there was no morning service, I went again to the riverside to gather violets and forget-me-nots, which on my return I deposited at the Rectory. There was service in the afternoon, and, as we came out, I persuaded the young ladies to wait in the churchyard, whilst I brought the basket to them; and they said again they would go and get violets themselves. In the evening, about an hour before the cloudless sunset, I went out with Thetis. I had never yet this year seen 'Bessy' on the terrace, but I had continued the habit of taking my evening walk along the footpath from which, in the past summer, I had seen her more than once 'come glimmering through the laurels'; and this beautiful evening there she was again in the white dress, straw hat, and green veil, and her little cousin with her. I was just about to jump a big fence when I saw them and, whilst I was gazing, the two 'Bessies' came down from the terrace and walked towards me across the field between the terrace and the footpath. They stopped half-way, and as they were now on neutral ground and not more than fifty yards off I determined to go to them. There was a gate into the field just opposite to them, and in a minute I and Thetis arrived. I think we must have been expected, but the object with which the young ladies had left the terrace was to pay a visit to a pet lamb with which I found them occupied. I did not remain long with them; and we conversed more by looks than by words. My 'Bessy' looked bright and happy, and the little 'Bessy' looked up at us with wistful intelligence in her dark eyes. The setting sun shone upon them both. I was standing with my back to it.

Monday, April 29th, the beautiful weather continued, and it seemed to me very likely that the young ladies would this day pay their visit to the violets. Now, if they did go, I knew very well the hour at which they would start and the road they would take. The hour would be not long after lunch, and they would go by the lane to get to which they must take the private road passing through the wood beyond the stable, a view of which road I could obtain, without being seen, from a certain point in the churchyard; and there I stationed myself, having my fishing tackle ready at the Rectory.

Presently I saw the procession pass, all five young ladies with the governess; and in a moment I was off. I picked up my tackle, and running at the top of my speed along the footpath that led to the London road, and along the footpath that led to Nanny Thorpe's cottage, and then, jumping a fence or two, I had just time to put the tackle ready together and begin fishing when the party arrived, issuing from the lane into the field beside the river. In a moment the five young ladies, each with a basket in her hand, were away from the governess and scrambling over the fence. They climbed the steep bank, and I was immediately among them. I spoke to all the others first and then joined 'Bessy'. The bank was so steep that she had sat down to gather violets, and I sat down beside her. She was on my right hand, and I fancy I can now see the falling ringlets and the soft blooming cheek. I put violets into her basket, and presently, seeing a forget-me-not, I picked it and gave it to her into her hand with a word or two which I am sure she understood. I had but just done this when the governess called out from the field below, 'Come home, young ladies, you have been here long enough'; she did not disguise her impatience to get them away. So away they went with such few violets as they had had time to get, and I was left to my fishing, the only result of which was that I broke my rod.

This was the last of the violets. On April 30th, I walked to the market town with Thetis and took tea with the kind aunt, returning late, quite happy and totally unprepared for the mortal wound that my now sanguine hopes were destined to receive on the very next day, which was the 1st of May—and 'Bessy's' birthday.

'This was the last of the violets'

CHAPTER IX

Union and Separation

WEDNESDAY, MAY 1st, 1839. On this day 'Bessy' was seventeen. What a Queen of May! So I thought that morning, and so have I thought ever since. Not shy and consumptive, like Tennyson's unfortunate May Queen, but a true and perfect embodiment of all the ideas associated with the ancient festival of love. At this date I did not even know the name of Tennyson, so that then I could not have made this comparison; not the less did I think of 'Bessy' on her seventeenth birthday as an ideal Queen of May.

The day passed with such thoughts. My tutor's wife had gone to bed, and I was alone with him, when he suddenly said, 'I have heard nothing from Cambridge about a second pupil; did——say anything to you about it?'

I told him exactly what had passed between me and the College Don.

'So, then, that was the meaning of that visit to Cambridge; you must leave my house.'

I answered that I must have left his house if he had obtained a second pupil, and I went and brought my father's letter. He turned red and said as he gave it back to me, 'I am afraid your father has not had the education of a gentleman'.

I said nothing, but I was becoming dangerous. We were standing on each side of a narrow table on which was a bed candle. I controlled myself, and he went on, somewhat inconsistently, 'Why did you not show me this letter when you got it? If you had done that, I should have given up the idea of a second pupil'. And then he agreed to reconsider the question of my leaving and let me know his decision in the morning.

When the morning came, he said that he was quite willing that I should remain, but that he had not been able to induce his wife to consent, adding very significantly and not unkindly, 'you have not been sufficiently careful since you came here to conciliate her'. He also added that he was sorry for the remark he had made about my father. So, then, our quarrel was over, but the lady was unappeasable, for reasons that had nothing to do with the question of a second pupil. What those reasons were I knew well enough. For a moment I thought of appealing to her and explaining how cruel she was; but the idea was no sooner entertained than dismissed. I felt I could tell her nothing that she did not know; and I was not at the end of my resources. There was a farmhouse in the village where they took in lodgers, and I asked my tutor if I could not lodge there and come to him daily for instruction, he paying the cost of my lodging out of receipts from my father. He said at once that he had no objection to such an arrangement, so I went to the farmhouse and made terms which he accepted without cavil. That very morning I made the move, and when on Friday, May 3rd, I went to dine at the Hall, I little dreamt that it was for the last time.

An impenetrable cloud of oblivion covers all the incidents of this evening, with the single exception of those relating to 'Bessy', and these shine out refulgent in the darkness. She was changed towards me, and seemed to look upon me as belonging to her, as indeed I did. Perhaps the forget-me-not had assured her of this. Whatever the cause there could be no mistake. As George Eliot says (*Middlemarch*, cap. 37), 'We mortals have sometimes divine moments in love', and these were divine moments that I now passed with 'Bessy'. Twice was I able to converse with her separately from the others. The first time was at the round table in the drawing room, and I remember her then saying to me, 'you *must* be a Tory'. I made no answer, but was deeply moved. They all knew that I was a great Radical, and these words, with the look with which they were accompanied, implied her knowledge that I wished to become a member of the family. What else was said at the round table I cannot remember, but later in the evening I got into a corner with her where we could not be overheard and there told her of what had happened between me and my tutor. She listened with the deepest interest, and then we talked of my going to college and what I was to do there. There is a passage in *Undine* describing a conversation of the knight with Bertalda, in which Fouqué says that the tone of the words was more significant than the words themselves; and such was the case between me and 'Bessy' in this our last conversation.

I fully believe that, if I had then made a formal declaration, it would have been received without the least surprise; but nothing of the kind seemed necessary as between her and me. She looked sure of me and happy in her confidence.

It will have been noticed that I have always written her name between quotation marks. The reason for this is that I have no distinct recollection of having addressed her as 'Bessy', but certainly I might have done so this evening, and probably did. I felt that we were in union.

The next morning it occurred to me that I ought myself to inform 'Bessy's' mother of my change of residence, so I called in the forenoon and found her in the drawing room with her eldest daughter and another lady. After the usual compliments I said that I wished to speak to her by herself. She instantly rose and led the way through the long drawing room, and then through the dining room to the library, and there took a seat and motioned me to a seat beside her. I said that I had come to inform her that in consequence of some differences between my tutor and myself we had arranged that I was to reside at the farmhouse whilst continuing to be his pupil until I went to Cambridge. The lady was equal to the occasion. She simply said, 'Mr.—— is our clergyman.' I then said that I had not the least intention of saying anything against him, but that, after all her kindness to me, I felt it to be right to inform her myself of my change of residence. She bowed in sign of acquiescence, and then rose and led the way back to the drawing room. I was charmed by her manner and her kindness. On my way back I met 'Bessy' and her younger sister and the two cousins in the garden.

On the Sunday morning, I received a letter from my mother, begging me to come home directly, as my father was ill and confined to bed, and wished for my company for a week or two. Coming out of church, I had a word with 'Bessy's' elder sister and told her this, and, in the afternoon, I called to enquire if I could be of service in taking anything to the Etonian, whom I intended to go and see. I was thanked, but nothing was wanted, and on Monday, May 5th, I went home. I found my father in bed, but getting better. I told him what had happened between me and my tutor and he instantly said, 'if you can't stay in the parson's house, you can't stay there at all.' What could I say? I shrank from speaking to him of my love and knew it would be of no use. I submitted, and concealed my anguish.

On Monday, the 13th, I paid my visit to the Etonian, travelling by the Great Western, which had just begun to carry passengers. I slept at Windsor. We walked together, and he dined with me and I remained with him in his room at the college as late as was allowed. He was very sorry to hear my news, and asked me if I would come to see them at the Hall during the summer holidays. I said that I should be delighted. In talking over the quarrel with my tutor I told him that I attributed the animosity of his wife to the slight I had put upon her by not taking her in to dinner at the Hall, to which he responded, 'We were all delighted'. We talked over the blind man's buff, and he asked me why I had turned back when I had so nearly caught 'Bessy'. This was an error on my part, for which I could not attempt any justification. I could only plead that it did not arise from indifference; but even now I did not tell him how serious was my attachment to his sister. We agreed to continue our correspondence, and I left him lulled into a false security by the prospect of a visit to the Hall in the course of the summer.

'We were standing on each side of a narrow table'

My hopes had indeed received a mortal wound, but they did not die yet. My father was now well again and had moved to his country house. 'Bessy's' little brother was at a school twelve miles off, and there I walked on Friday, the 17th, on a hot day and along a dusty road. This clever little boy was glad to see me, and I entertained him at the village inn. On Monday, the 27th, I left London for the North of England, it having been arranged that I was to pay a visit to some relatives there,[1] and, on my way, to settle with my tutor and pick up my belongings. I travelled by night outside the coach and arrived at my lodgings early in the morning. I settled with my tutor, and then went to the Hall to say good-bye, having now been absent three weeks. I was received with great kindness. No explanation was necessary, the Etonian having written; and when I asked for the young ladies I was told that they were all in the schoolroom, and that I could go to them.

I found the three sisters sitting in a row before the governess, beside whom I took a seat. She was to my right, and opposite to me came the youngest sister to my left, then 'Bessy', and then the eldest sister. I am thus particular in my description, not that I have any memorandum to guide me but because I feel myself obliged to describe carefully what I still see so distinctly. My diary merely says that '"Bessy" was looking very pale and ill', as indeed she was. And she looked not only pale and ill, but also unhappy.

Conversation was somewhat difficult, but I availed myself of the circumstances, and enquired about the young ladies' studies. This loosened the tongue of the governess, who ended by saying that she would like them to be examined in my presence; a safe enough suggestion, as she no doubt thought, now that I was going away. 'That would be of no use', said 'Bessy', shaking her head; 'we should not be able to do anything; we should all be thinking of him'. The governess uttered an exclamation of annoyance, and a dead silence ensued. 'Bessy' did not change countenance, nor did her sisters. Presently, I said a few words of farewell and then tore myself away, satisfied that 'Bessy's' white face and sad fixed look were caused by grief at our separation. 'Had she been crying?' I could not help asking myself the question.

CHAPTER X

Hope Bleeding to Death

THAT MISERABLE AFTERNOON, Tuesday, May 28th, I went to say good-bye to Nanny Thorpe, taking with me a pair of tortoiseshell spectacles, which, with some trouble, I had procured for her, and which, I was glad to find, exactly suited her. I found out, as far back as the past summer, that her sight was defective; but my glasses did not suit her, and I did not know what to do until I consulted an optician in London who had recently sold me a pair of opera glasses. He gave me a few eye-pieces for trial, and I had brought these with me when I returned to the Rectory after Christmas. One of them suited, and now with the spectacles I made my dear 'Bessy's' nurse happy, and added, I hope, to the comfort of her declining years. Then I paid a farewell visit to the keeper, walked about with him, and took a glass of ale at his house; and I did not forget Thetis. Finally, I fell asleep over my supper at the farmhouse in a state of exhaustion.

Next morning I received a note from 'Bessy's' elder sister, asking me to call to receive a parcel which she would give me to deliver for her mother at York; so I went to the door opening into the end of the lane, and there the young lady met me. I expressed my grief at my departure in a manner I had not been able to do in the schoolroom. She knew perfectly well that I referred more to her sister than to herself in what I said, but we had always been the best of friends, and she was indeed very charming, as well as most estimable.

I walked to the market town to meet the coach. It was a glorious evening, reminding me of the evening of the two 'Bessies' and the pet lamb; and, as I passed by the park lodge, I stopped for some minutes and leant over the gate in contemplation, with the conscious intention of fixing the scene in my memory for the rest of my life. The sun was behind me, and I looked with melancholy admiration at the great trees, their long shadows over the grass, and the distant view.[1]

I took leave of the good, kind aunt at the market town, and the same evening I wrote to the Etonian. It was a terrible night journey to York on the top of the coach. I arrived chilled to the bone with the east wind and covered with dust, and, having discharged my commision went to the Minster and museum, and walked along the Ouse as far as Bishopsthorpe, which interested me greatly.

Next day I went on to join my friends in the extreme North. There I learnt the rudiments of fly-fishing, and it was not until Saturday, the 6th of July, that I resumed my studies under the care of a great scholar and most amiable gentleman[2] who took me into his house at Cambridge. On Sunday, the 7th, I called on 'Bessy's' uncle. He was very kind, and from time to time I continued to see him during the whole of my residence at the university. Sometimes I took wine with him, sometimes he came to my rooms to take wine with me, and on other occasions we walked together. From him I gathered scraps of information about the family at the Hall, and I suspect that he knew well enough the state of my affections, although I never spoke to him explicity on the subject. I find by my diary that on July 19th I wrote some poetry to 'Bessy' and took tea with her uncle; and, hearing from him that he was going on a visit to the Hall, I told him all the particulars of my quarrel with my tutor, and begged him to put me right with the family, which he promised to do.

'On the top of the coach'

I was thinking of the invitation which the Etonian had spoken of; but, although our correspondence continued, the summer holidays passed and it never came. And now my heart began to sink. Looking back to this time, I wonder how I can have been so mad as to expect such an invitation. Had I even really been the eldest son and heir of a millionaire (and by this time it must have been known that I was not), I had no right to hope that the invitation would come. I had not declared myself, and it would have been like throwing the young lady at my head. But I did not make these reflections at the time, and there is an entry in my diary on September 16th saying how very 'wretched' I was at the holidays having passed without any invitation.

After this, my correspondence with the Etonian slackened, that is to say, on his part, for I always answered his letters quickly, whilst he became slower and slower in replying to mine. Still I did not give up the hope of hearing from him until February 16, 1840, when I wrote in my diary: 'Had tea with C. (a very intimate friend) and told him about my love affair with her I shall never see again. I cannot write her name. Her brother has cut my correspondence. O God!'

The occasion of this reference to the Etonian was that his uncle had just told me that he had received a letter from him. I had long been waiting for one, and I knew now that no more would come. But I am going on too fast

Whilst I was at the house of my new tutor previous to my matriculation at Trinity, I occupied a large double-bedded room, the tenant of the second bed being another pupil,[3] to whom I soon became attached and took into my confidence as he took me into his. He had only moderate abilities, his charm being in his sweet disposition and expression. He was the last remaining scion of a family as old as the family at the Hall, and bore the name of the village he came from. A dissipated grandfather had dilapidated the ancestral estate, and the one idea of this fair youth was to restore it by good conduct and good management. All this he told me, and I used to relieve myself by talking to him about my love.

The curtains of our beds were white. Just about daybreak, one morning in August, between sleeping and waking, I fancied that I saw 'Bessy' dressed in white, with the white face and sad fixed look that had continued to haunt me ever since our parting in the schoolroom. I started, and saw it was only the curtain of the bed opposite, but the impression, though only momentary, was most vivid.

At this time also I made the acquaintance of a very singular and interesting character[4] who used to frequent my tutor's hospitable house and find solace in the society of his wife and family. He was a little, slender, pale, dreamy-looking man, one of the finest classical scholars that Cambridge ever produced, and had been prevented by religious scruples from retaining a fellowship at Trinity. He had an extremely refined and delicate nature and exquisite literary taste. His valuable commentaries on Shakespeare were published after his death.[5]

I did not at this time take him into my confidence, but, after I became an undergraduate, he used frequently to come to my rooms of an evening; and on one of these occasions, after we had had our fill of poetry and Greek, I opened my heart to him, and he is the only person to whom I ever repeated 'Bessy's' little speech in the schoolroom, ending with the words, 'we should all be thinking of him'. He then said, after a pause, that this incident reminded him of Fouqué's description of Undine before she had a soul.

On the day of the winter solstice, December 21st, being then at home in London, I went for a walk in the Regent's Park with my favourite sister and a little brother. 'Bessy's' cousins lived near the Regent's Park, and I had a presentiment that I should see them. We met them in the broad avenue, one on each side of a lady, who was, I presume, their mother. The little one was on my side, and knew me, and nodded to me. After they had passed, my sister asked me what was the matter with me. She said I turned all manner of colours. And on the 31st December, in the same place, the same thing happened, except that the elder sister was not present, and three times I passed the little one. The first time she did not see me, but twice she nodded in her arch manner. So ended 1839, with hope not quite dead, and love stronger than ever.

On January 16, 1840, I went to the Regent's Park alone, and, being alone, it was my intention to have spoken to the 'little Bessy' in case I saw her, but I looked for her in vain. The next day I returned to Cambridge and went immediately to see the good uncle, but he had no news for me. He had not seen any of the family during the vacation. My diary tells me that on the 21st I walked in the direction of dear——, giving the name of the village. On February 4th, I wrote my last letter to the Etonian, asking him why he had never answered my former letters. On February 15th, his uncle took tea with me, and I showed him an accidental likeness of 'Bessy's' younger sister. He laughed and told me to send it to her at once and finish the matter. And now came an absolute cessation of information and a steady growth of despondency. I became desperate, and, when the examination at the end of the May term was over, an examination in which I acquitted myself with much credit, I determined to go and see 'Bessy'.

On Friday, June 12th, I arrived at the market town, and went to see the good aunt, but she was away, and her servant told me that the family at the Hall were all in London, with the exception of the youngest daughter and the youngest son, who had broken his leg. I was mad, but I walked off to the village, called on my old tutor, and then at the Hall, where I saw the little lady, now much grown and looking more serious than she used to, and from her I obtained her mother's address, which was an hotel in Dover Street. I had some visits to pay to relations in the country and some fly-fishing to do, and I did not get home until Friday, June 26.

The next day I went to the opera, where my mother had a box; but, except whilst Taglioni[6] was dancing, I paid very little attention to the stage. Opposite me I saw 'Bessy', looking more lovely than ever, with her two lovely cousins. They were in the front row of a large box, twice the size of any other box in the house. I think it was the old royal box. I always made good use of my opera glasses, and soon found them out. They did not use opera glasses, and I think never saw me. I thought of going to their box, but how could I do so when it was full of strangers? Had 'Bessy's' mother been of the party, I should have gone. As it was, I only went to the door and looked through the little window in the door; I could not venture to go in.

And having ladies to take care of, I could not look out for 'Bessy' when the performance was over.

On the following Wednesday, July 1, I called in Dover Street, and was told that the whole party had left on the previous Thursday. My diary says: 'How then, can I have seen 'Bessy' at the opera on Saturday?'

But I had made no mistake. How could I? She had been left in London with her married aunt for a reason that was soon to be explained.

The first time I saw her uncle at Cambridge after the long vacation he told me she was engaged to be married. She had been taken to Almack's, where she caused a sensation, and had captivated, at her first ball, a young baronet[7] with an immense landed estate. I said nothing, but the good uncle saw my deep distress and said something with the view of enabling me to bear it. But that something was in depreciation of 'Bessy', and it passed me unheeded, and indeed was not very deserving of attention, however kindly intended. It was merely to the effect that her beauty would not last.

I was not surprised; nor was I so utterly unreasonable as to think I had the slightest cause for complaint. All the same, I had received a tremendous blow.

Very soon after, 'Bessy' was married.

CHAPTER XI

The Silver Shape

I MUST NOW go back a little. I have already said that 'Bessy's' white face and sad fixed look haunted me for some time after our separation. Presently, however, she came back to me smiling and beautiful, such as I had seen her from the Coronation Day up to our last and only unhappy interview. I never actually saw her apparition, but this mental vision was so distinct as to be little distinguishable from the apparition of a person, such as, once in the course of my life, I actually beheld.

I could always see 'Bessy' when I wished, and, very often she came to me when I was not thinking of her. It frequently happened that some young girl in the distance would take her form for a moment of hallucination which would occur before I had time to reflect. I sometimes saw ringlets like 'Bessy's', and then I always saw herself. Her image became part of my existence, and neither time nor circumstances made any difference. My hope died, but still 'Bessy' smiled. She married, and still she smiled. I ceased to connect her with the realities of life, but she belonged to a paradise from which I had been expelled, and to which my thoughts and longings continually returned.

I always intended to marry, but I made up my mind that I must do so without looking for the unapproachable charm of my lost love, and without experiencing a tithe of the emotion which I felt in thinking of her. Such is the best account I can give of the 'silver shape' that so persistently attended me.

When I left Cambridge I travelled and I find in the diary, which I kept during my journey, the following passages: 'Rome, May 8th, 1843. Called on B., who went with me to the Vatican and pointed out the best things to me, but half way through he told me that "Bessy"—as she once was and still is to me—was coming to the Continent, and afterwards I saw nothing more, which he soon perceived and left off playing the cicerone.' Again: 'Rome, May 26th. Visited by a vision of 'Bessy', etc., scene after scene with long-forgotten incidents. Very painful—could I but write when in these visions!'[1]

I did not go to the Bar. When I returned from the Continent I took charge, at my father's request, of a manufactory of which he was the principal owner; and the time now came when I decided to marry, the business being exceedingly prosperous, and my inclinations being utterly adverse to celibacy. I saw several young ladies who pleased me to the full extent that I conceived it possible for me to be pleased, and might easily have made my choice very coolly, although never for money. In one case, I very nearly put the question because the young lady had ringlets like 'Bessy's'. In another case, although I said nothing, I certainly behaved very badly, although not so badly as must have been supposed. I went so far as to ask my father's permission to engage myself. He opposed my wishes most violently, and my affection had not sufficient strength to carry me over the obstacle.

Things were in this position when one day in the spring of 1844, being then just 23 years old, I suddenly discovered that 'Bessy's' image had become less frequent in its appearances and less distinct; and this was the first circumstance that led me to suspect the altered state of my inclinations. This was no mere question between a reality and a vision. Other realities had had no effect upon the vision, but, bit by bit, during the last few months, another influence, another appearance, had been gradually creeping over and covering up the image of 'Bessy', which never disappeared (it is with me still) but, from this time forward, became less distinct. I had seen the lady who, three years later, became my wife.

Three years later! Obstacles that did not proceed from herself I swept away, but she was hard to win and of her I shall say no more than is necessary for the proper filling up of the present narrative. We lived together for 42 years, and I am one of the few men who can say that he married the woman that he loved best.

Love may be of various kinds and degrees. The foundation of love between the sexes is, of course, that powerful and universal natural force that draws them together; but to this may be added the feeling of kindness produced by goodness and amiability, and to these two elements, so conducive to union, may again be added the overpowering charm of intellectual sympathy.

In my love for 'Bessy' the two first elements were combined, but, in my love for my wife all three. She could never have said to me, 'You *must* be a Tory'. We thought alike on all important questions, whether of affairs of state or of religion, and this agreement was a genuine coincidence of independent judgments. And here I must say, in passing, that we never became Gladstonians. Mr Gladstone's 'Russianism' drove us out of the Liberal ranks long before the Unionist secession. Through all changes of circumstances in the body politic my wife and I kept together and worked together to the last. An extreme nobility was her main characteristic, and she drew around us men who resembled her in this, one of whom still remains to me and is the best friend that ever man had.

In her youth, my wife was quite as beautiful as 'Bessy', but in a totally different style. Slightly taller, somewhat more strongly built, with dark silky hair, and broad intelligent brows, a clear brunette in complexion, with large dark beautiful eyes, the most beautiful I ever beheld, and with a voice the tenderness of which was at times indescribable, she aroused in me the utmost intensity of emotion of which my nature was capable. But still she did not quite efface the 'silver shape'.

After my marriage, as before, I still continued to treasure the old pocket book, and still, from time to time, would I imagine myself with 'Bessy' among the violets or in other circumstances such as I have described. I told my wife all about it, and, not long after we were married, I took her with me to see the Rectory and the Hall. I had long ago forgiven my tutor and even his wife; we found them with many infants, and then went on to the Hall, where we saw the new owner, 'Bessy's' eldest brother, his wife and children being absent. He was very cordial, and I could see that he was agreeably impressed by my wife as she was by him. He gave a good account of his sister, from whom he was expecting a visit. Thus my wife knew everything; but whilst she never doubted that 'Bessy' was as charming as I said, and that I had loved her as I said, never could I bring my wife to believe that my affection had been returned. Whenever I hinted that such was my belief, she would say quietly that she thought I must have deceived myself—an opinion which was not without influence upon what afterwards occurred.

The end of my life is clouded by misfortune. I am one of those to whom may be applied the saying of Solon:

'Call no man happy till he dies'.

And yet, I cannot but look back to much of my life with very great pleasure. As to this matter of retrospection, my experience is contradictory of Dante's famous saying, and goes rather to support Byron's less known words, 'And come what may, I have been blest'.

What can take away from me the happy memory of certain sunny midsummer weeks in 1866? I had now been married

19 years; I was 45, and in the very fullness of manly vigour; my wife had recovered from an illness that had threatened her life, and was still so beautiful that, although she was now 39, I could often perceive admiration in the eyes of those who saw her; my affairs had been so prosperous that I had been able to buy a small but most beautiful landed estate[2] (bounded on one side by one of the best salmon rivers in Great Britain) without troubling my father; and finally I had three good children, a boy in his fifteenth year at Eton,[3] a younger boy at Harrow, and a daughter in her seventeenth year. Our Etonian had been taken ill, and my wife and I went to Windsor to look after him, and, when his convalescence was well established, we took him away with us to spend a fortnight at an hotel on the banks of the Thames which goes by the name of 'Skindle's'; and there our daughter joined us. I will give the best history that I can of this happy fortnight, and of the incident that marked its conclusion; and must begin with a little topography.

Skindles Hotel faces the London road just before you get to Maidenhead Bridge, and just above the bridge and separated from the river by a very pretty lawn stands the new part of the hotel intended for the accommodation of resident visitors, and connected with the old part by a covered way. This is a two-storey building, the bedrooms being on the upper floor, and the ground floor consisting of four comfortable sitting rooms, each with a large glass window door opening on to the lawn at the same level. There is a stone stair from which you can step from the lawn into a boat, and to the left, close to the bridge, is a boathouse where any description of pleasure craft can be hired. About half a mile above comes Boulter's Lock, then Cliveden, Cookham, and Marlow. In this new part of the hotel did we settle ourselves just a fortnight before the Ascot Week, and, as the whole of the rooms were let for the Ascot Week, we had to turn out on the previous Saturday.

From first to last the weather was magnificent, and we made

the most of it. We arranged with a boatman to hold himself at our disposition, and every day we were on the water; not always the ladies, but always I and my son. We did some fishing, but, after a few days, gave up fishing for rowing, on account of the intense heat. I had learnt to row at Cambridge, my son was one of the best oars at Eton, and even the lazy beer-drinking boatman said that 'rowing was better than sitting frying in a punt catching gudgeon'. The opening of the pores by exercise brought relief, and we pulled vigorously in the blazing sun.

'Every day we were on the water'

One day we went to Marlow, but our point was generally Cookham, and well did we learn to know the Cliveden woods and the double shadows at the head of Cliveden reach. Sometimes we had friends with us who came from London for the day. A row on these waters in fine weather with good company is indeed a supreme enjoyment. Every boat on the Thames seemed to be engaged these sunny days, and the parties of young people continually passing added not a little to the beauty of the scene and to our enjoyment. An occasional steam-launch was the only drawback; they ought not to be allowed on this part of the Thames.

Very often young ladies were rowing, and sometimes 'came two young lovers lately wed'. And, as the weather grew hotter and hotter, appeared occasional punts (occupied by loving couples) comfortably fitted up with a cushion on the seat and a carpet on the floor; and these did not travel much. They were generally moored in some quick current under the shade, and there they would remain long after sunset. One moonlight night I saw a loving couple in one of these punts who seemed to have no intention of moving. But we never remained late on the water. My wife could not stay out late, and we always returned in good time for the elegant little dinner served up to us in our pretty sitting room, and for the cider-cup for which Skindles is so justly famous. Dinner would be over a little before sunset, and then I would go out on the lawn; but the ladies would stay indoors and the glass door would be shut, as my wife was still rather delicate. At first there were other visitors at the hotel, but they all went away, and at the beginning of our second week we had Skindles to ourselves.

On the Wednesday of this second week I went to London and returned very late. Then said my wife to me, 'Lady D——[4] is here.' I was incredulous. 'Yes,' continued my wife, 'Mrs Skindles gave me her name; she arrived in the afternoon and walked round this way and looked in at our window.' I remained incredulous; but next morning when Mrs Skindles came to take our orders for the day, she repeated the name to me, and seeing that I knew it, added, 'a nice lady'. The last time I had seen 'Bessy' was at the opera in 1840; I had never since made any attempt to see her, and now, after twenty-six years, we were close together.

I had followed her fortunes. I knew that she had been greatly admired in London society after her marriage, as well as before it. I knew that she had a family, and I knew that now for some years she had been a widow. It might be reasonably expected that I should have eagerly embraced this most singular opportunity for renewing our acquaintance. On the contrary, the presence of the opportunity overthrew my reason so completely for the time being that during the whole of the two days that we were close together I could never command sufficient self-possession to make myself known.

'How shall I be received?' was the question that distracted me. I was sure of civility and even more; but would there be any recognition, express or implied, of the nature of our former relations? Should I find in Lady D—— any trace of my lost 'Bessy'? Might not the great world and its conventionalities have completely spoiled the child of nature that I remembered? What of Undine would be left? Might not my wife's opinion receive confirmation? The 'silver shape' came between us. Might I not destroy it? 'Bessy' seemed to say to me, 'I am not Lady D——. If you speak to her, I shall go away'. Such things did I revolve in my burning heart and remained in a state of irresolution.

All the time I wanted to speak but my courage failed me. My wife advised me to send my card to Lady D——, and ask when I could speak to her. It was good advice, but I answered that I would take my chance of a meeting on the lawn; and, on the Thursday, we did meet on the lawn more than once; but I always kept at such a distance from the lady that recognition was impossible. She had with her a daughter, and her I did not avoid, a very beautiful girl about the same age as my daughter, but who did not remind me of her mother, having dark hair and dark sparkling eyes. She had also her eldest son up from Eton, about the same age as my son, who knew him by sight and by name, but did not happen to have his acquaintance. Their pursuits differed. One was in the boats and the other a cricketer; in Eton language one was a 'wet Bob' and the other a 'dry Bob'; and so they had not met. It was a further curious coincidence that Lady D—— and my wife had identical parasols, mauve lined with white.

A friend joined Lady D——'s party, and they took boat as we did on this day; and, in the evening, when I came out on the lawn after dinner, they took boat again, and did not return until it was nearly quite dark, when they found me still pacing up and down the lawn. All this day I carefully avoided Lady D——, and she must have seen that I did so.

Friday passed much in the same way until the evening, when, my son having returned to Eton in his skiff, I was alone on the lawn after dinner. Then I saw Lady D—— go with her party to the boat stair, but she did not get into the boat. She said something to them, as I could see by her manner, and then turned back and took a seat in her sitting room close to the open glass door.

Had she seen my embarrassment, and did she do this on purpose to encourage me to speak to her? I am convinced that she did. She must have known who I was. Mrs Skindles must have given her our name just as she gave her name to us. Her son would know my son by sight and by name; a good oar at Eton is well known; and then she must have heard of my wife from her brother. She must also have noticed how carefully I had avoided her.

But all these reflections came too late. Had I, at the time, had even the faintest suspicion that Lady D—— was sitting at the open glass door expecting me to come and speak to her, I should have been by her side in an instant; but no such suspicion entered my disordered mind. I was fully sensible of the value of the opportunity, but still continued to pace up and down the lawn in a state of irresolution. Sometimes I drew nearer to Lady D——, near enough to see her luminous eyes shining in the growing darkness, and then I drew away again; and I was still thinking that now I really would go to her and still pacing up and down the lawn, when the clash of oars, followed by the sound of youthful voices, broke the silence of the night. The boating party had returned; the opportunity was lost.

CHAPTER XII

A Few Last Words

IT IS A common practice with writers of history to enter into speculation as to what might have happened had the actors in the events related done something different from what they actually did; and in writing one's own history it is not quite possible to avoid falling into reflections of this description. But to such reflections I shall give no expression except upon one single point. What would have happened had I availed myself of the singularly favourable opportunity which came to me for renewing in mature years my acquaintance with the lady who had been 'the idol of my youth'? Is it possible that the result could have been pain and disappointment?

I have long been convinced of the contrary. What was it that drew me to her so strongly in early days? Not merely the charm of youth and beauty. Added to this was the open heart and amiable disposition which caused her to be beloved by all who knew her, and which gave to her smile its transcendent beauty. Should I have been disenchanted? Should we not have found that we were still friends? Would not she and my wife have become friends? Might not our children have become friends? Such were the reflections that gradually obtained the mastery over the unreasoning tumult of my emotions and brought with them a life-long regret at my fatuity. And these reflections were destined to receive a striking confirmation.

A few years ago, finding myself, on a public occasion in the company of Lady D——'s eldest son, I obtained an introduction and conversed with him for fully an hour. I told him all that I possibly could about my year's residence at the Rectory; I spoke of myself as being still most grateful for all the kindness I had received from the family at the Hall; and I sent through him my kind regards to all the survivors (not many) and more especially to his mother. He promised to deliver all my messages and, I have no doubt, did so.

We discoursed further on some very important public matters as to which he expressed himself with a good sense and good feeling which I have rarely seen equalled. He has already done good service to his country, and is looked to do more. How it moved my heart to look at him and hear him! He had his mother's features and voice and manner, and even something of her smile. Then did I regret more than ever that I had lost the opportunity of renewing our acquaintance. But I could not intrude my old age upon hers. She would get my message, and it would probably recall to her the days of our youth. I could do no more.

She died when the violets were last in bloom, and I lay down the pencil, not the pen (I can now only write in bed with a pencil), on this 28th of June, 1894, the fifty-sixth anniversary of Victoria's Coronation Day, and of the day on which I first met my early love at the dance on the village green.

THE END

Postscript

By Edmund Esdaile

George Crawshay (1821–1896) was my great-grandfather. Originally destined for the Bar, he had just successfully completed the final examinations when the accidental death in 1843* of his brother-in-law, Francis William Stanley, created a vacancy in the firm of Hawks, later Hawks, Crawshay & Co., of Gateshead; the widow transferred her interest to her father and brother, who joined the firm.

George's father, also George, was the third and youngest son of William Crawshay the elder of Cyfarthfa in South Wales; he worked there and in the London office. The Gateshead firm was important and became more so; George's obituarist in *The Times* of 23 March 1896, writing presumably of its heyday in his time, wrote: 'altogether it is said that . . . [it] turned out 45,000 tons of bridges, with 15 large lighthouses, and many other works', the High Level Bridge at Newcastle, Lendal Bridge in York, and the bridges over the Hoogli and the Golden Horn among them.**

---

* The accident was instant and unpredictable. Frank Stanley was out riding alone, sudden rain came and a clap of loud thunder; the horse shied and threw him and he died.

** The bridge over the Golden Horn had a much more complex history than this phrase implies.

The technical inventiveness which led to the Industrial Revolution—an event for which there was no precedent—found expression in an England whose towns had for centuries been ordered by craftsmen and tradesmen with their journeymen and apprentices and whose countryside had no less anciently been ordered by lords of the manor and yeomen with peasants and ancillary craftsmen in smithy, wheelwright's yard, cobbler's shop and so forth; the Crawshays until after 1750 were yeomen from Normanton near Sheffield.

If, to quote the old saying, Jack was not (and indeed is not) as good as his master, the industrious apprentice could (and did) become so—Richard Crawshay for one, who after just such a start in London founded the family fortunes in Merthyr Tydfil. And here, as Malkin records in his *History of South Wales*, one of his ordinary workers, by name Watkin George, contrived a great and useful wheel and by otherwise applying his efforts ended as a partner in Richard Crawshay's firm. As for housing, thrown up higgledy-piggledy as folk migrated there for work, the consequently very bad conditions were being supplanted as early as 1806, when Malkin wrote, by planned improvements. In brief, these founding fathers of industry were individuals of independent, energetic and competitive spirit, at their worst as bad as they have been painted, at their best, as in the cases of Josiah Wedgwood, Jedediah Strutt and later Sir Titus Salt, men still deserving our honour; and I suspect that with their faults and their virtues the early Crawshays, although (as George allows and as Lady Charlotte Guest perceived) they could be outspoken, harsh and even eccentric, were not, despite their failings, among the worst of their kind.[1]

All such men were alike, however, in being very much masters, each in his own right. Yet if combinations of workers had been suspect (and history had not shewn apprentices to be uniformly orderly), and if each master so cherished his own independence as to mistrust the idea of a masters' combination, among these same masters were in due course to be found radicals not unsympathetic towards the Chartists; George Crawshay's future father-in-law, the surgeon Sir John Fife,[2] was the radical mayor of Newcastle to whom fell the duty in 1839 of suppressing the Chartist riots there and whose firmness and justice availed to restore order without further embittering those whom he suppressed.

It was at this time, before in all probability the Fifes and the Crawshays had ever met, that 'Bessy' said to George at Flintham, knowing him to be a great Radical, 'You *must* be a Tory'. Of the coincidence no hint is given, for it was a coincidence only in retrospect; but the unrest was common knowledge and clearly 'Bessy' was thinking in terms of their two family backgrounds. The unspoken trends at this crucial moment of both young people's minds cannot be mistaken.

George Crawshay was in two entirely distinct ways a transitional figure. In the fourth generation of industrial wealth he eventually graduated to the ranks of the landed gentry to which by birth he did not belong. The process, although none guessed it, began at Flintham; and when one remembers *The Newcomes* (Clive Newcome in Chapter VII of that novel[3] may well be collated with Crawshay's Chapter IV) *A Silver Shape* is seen as documenting Thackeray's imaginative perception. Secondly, although Crawshay became and remained not a barrister but an industrialist, he did not as a result of landed status coupled with prosperity lose all the beliefs of his youth; he never lost his interest in people, including his work-people. It was for purely political reasons that little by little he became disillusioned with Gladstone's Liberal party.

But from the late 1840s he was for a quarter of a century prominent with others, among them his friend Cobden and also Bright (one of the few with whom he failed to establish friendship), as a partisan in every Liberal cause. Partitioned Poles, rebellious Hungarians, assaulted Danes he championed; Garibaldi he knew personally; the Crimean War, the Indian

Mutiny, the Chinese and Afghan Wars engaged his active attention; half French though he was, he at first thought the French at fault in 1871 until the Germans by their immoderation forfeited his sympathy. Although now forgotten, he must have been a valuable ally to those who thought as he did; he contributed not only time and money but also wide culture, observant travels, linguistic ability, social gifts and a significant acquaintance, a combination to which only some of the others could equally well aspire. To say this is not to urge that he and they were right; not to say it would be false to fact.

Politics were his great public interest and above all, foreign policy. From this arose his eventual rejection of Gladstone, whose preference of Russia to Turkey he considered prejudiced, short-sighted and on a long view dangerous. This was not merely theoretical. He knew Turkey and leading Turks of the reforming party there; he liked and trusted them; in 1872 he wrote valuable letters from there to his wife; and here in England he not only acted as Turkish Consul in Newcastle but was also a friend and supporter of the diplomat and politician David Urquhart (1805–1877)[4], who shared his views and whom he prominently assisted in organizing Foreign Affairs Committees in major English towns.

In short, his original plan to become a barrister was undoubtedly right and English political life may have lost a distinguished figure when it was abandoned; but in the event his Liberalism slowly faded. Not that he neglected his business; far from it. In the boom years of Victorian prosperity it throve. He worked at it; and he was the opposite of a remote, impersonal employer. Wealth enabled him to lead a busy public life, to indulge his varied hobbies, to bring up his children on the estate which he bought, to enjoy field sports, but also to help and encourage others, whoever they were, provided only that they needed encouragement and help—the last years of his gifted and unhappy Cambridge friend Sidney Walker, eased mainly by Praed and a small college pension, provided a case in point. But if his open-handedness became publicly known it was not from his choice but because willy-nilly these things do not always remain private. It is to Walker's notice in *The D.N.B.* that I owe knowledge of George Crawshay's contribution; there is no hint of it in the papers (see notes, Chapter x, n.5).

Half French by birth and bilingual, he had a flair for languages and retained both his classics and his mathematics. He was of course much affected by the Romantic Movement but also, to quote a much earlier writer (Sir Henry Chauncy), 'he would be very free, brisk and merry in all companies',[5] of which he left ample evidence in the very readable manuscript journals which he kept in Germany, central Europe, Greece and Italy. He contributed regularly prose and verse to *The Newcastle Chronicle* and his prose is consistently better, with one exception, than is the verse which he wrote with facility but without distinction; the exception is a sprightly verse-drama about hunting called *A Run with the Tyndale Hounds*. He was interested in and apparently wrote about botany, writings of which I know nothing. He had excellent taste in pictures and a perceptive appreciation of them. No doubt with Urquhart's approval but also aware of what he himself had observed he installed in his home the first Turkish bath ever seen in Great Britain which, however, I believe to have been narrowly preceded in south-west Ireland. In Gateshead he served three times as Mayor and he took a lively interest both in the Mechanics' Institute there (shades of Watkin George?) and in the Polytechnic at Newcastle, even lecturing to and otherwise addressing the students.

Perhaps there were those in politics who regarded his and Urquhart's Foreign Affairs Committees, to name but one activity, as a busybody's quirk; there were certainly commercial leaders on Tyneside who viewed with suspicion all this fluent versatility, which they thought an unsuitable distraction from the serious practice of business; for when after years of constant prosperity the works of this most generous man were forced to close some comments were shamefully ungenerous and neglectful of his widely beneficial and selfless service of others. He retired to Sussex, to my grandparents' house, and there after a short illness he died, never repining for himself but saddened for the three and a half thousand workpeople whom he had once employed.

Why did the works fail? The proximate cause, I was told, was as in other cases new developments in making steel. Iron had always been the Crawshays *métier*; steel no doubt would find its own niche in the iron industry; and George Crawshay, a conscientious head of his firm, was not alone in so misjudging. But he was surely vulnerable on other grounds. Not only was he a Crawshay of the fourth generation, to whom iron and prosperity seemed an automatic pair; multifarious outside interests had always occupied him and in business his acumen may well have suffered. 'I told you so'—such in a phrase was the attitude of some on Tyneside and it ill became them; but they were not, it can be suggested, wholly mistaken.

Yet in the last analysis the hallmark of George Crawshay was gratitude for being alive and well in a wonderful world and the memory which he left is sweet. He would have approved Dr Johnson's dictum that it is better to live rich than to die rich. His old age may have been 'clouded by misfortune', but how many of the misfortunate are grateful enough at the end to count themselves, as in Chapter XI he did, blest? 'I would sooner have sat next to him at dinner than any man I ever knew,' said my grandmother's friend and contemporary Mrs Sidney Streatfeild. He did much good; and one cannot but feel distaste for the tone of the carping comments uttered by lesser men, a minority but wounding, who were wiser in their generation than the children of light.

But that is not quite all.

In the last chapter of *A Silver Shape* he wonders what would have happened if in his forties he had seized the opportunity of renewing his acquaintance with 'the idol of my youth. Would not she and my wife have become friends? Might not our children have become friends?'

By a fate as inscrutable and singular as that which removed him from the threshold of a legal and political career his wish, without anyone being for some long time aware of it, has been fulfilled; the circumstances have differed, the individuals have differed, but it has been fulfilled none the less.

The following paragraphs complete the story.

After my grandmother's death in 1936 George Crawshay's papers came to my father and slumbered undisturbed for years on our shelves. Once or twice at long intervals my father referred briefly to this tale of early love as 'charming', but we were a busy family, nobody pursued the subject and nothing was done. At the beginning of the 1950s, however, I came to know one of the two friends to whom this edition of *A Silver Shape* is dedicated and to meet, in due course to know, the other.

The Crawshay papers having remained undisturbed, no thought of a past link between our geographically separated families occurred to any of us. More years passed and then belatedly I studied the papers, identified Flintham and conveyed the news there and to Henry Thorold.* Later still came the decision to edit the narrative for publication.

The decision was mine, as mine too must be the responsibility for any errors and imperfections; but without the hospitality, talk and encouragement of the other two the task of enacting it would have been barely possible besides devoid of most of its meaning. It so happens that with a singular and indeed humbling aptness I am George Crawshay's senior male great-grandchild (he left no grandson of his name) and so by descent

* When I told Henry and his mother the latter at once exclaimed 'Then you are our honorary cousin!' Mrs Thorold is now dead, but her phrase, incorporated in the dedication, salutes her memory.

his representative; and it has fallen to me to accompany him back to a Hildyard and a Thorold, to welcome him with them in their Midland countryside which he never forgot and at the same time to know him as I had never known him before. He has now been dead for over eighty years; but we have all felt the gentle touch of his friendship.

The three strands no longer lie loose and forgotten. They have been picked up, brushed and finally interwoven; and we grandchildren's children[6] in our generation have been at one in doing this, therein, as was perceived only when the task was nearly finished, fulfilling his wish. When next the spring flowers are in bloom I shall, God willing, visit the churchyard in Sussex where he and my grandparents lie buried and in the name of us all lay over him a posy of freshly gathered violets.

GEORGE CRAWSHAY

From a drawing in *The Newcastle Daily Chronicle*

Historical Notes

CHAPTER I

(1) *A French lady &c.* She was Louise, daughter of Georges Dufaud and his wife Gabrielle, *née* Garnier des Garets. See *Le Roman des Dufaud* by their descendant Denise le Mallier (Delayance, La Charité-sur-Loire, 1971). Georges Dufaud, besides being an iron-master, was, as George Crawshay says, scientifically distinguished in his own right; there is also in Mme le Mallier's book a good deal about the Crawshays; and not the least interesting part is that in which we learn about the period during and after the Napoleonic wars, including at least a hint of industrial spying.

(2) *Founded a peerage.* This was Sir Benjamin Hall, Lord Llanover, First Commissioner of Works and the 'Big Ben', after whom, as I established, the bell was named. Lady Llanover edited the writings of Mrs Delany.

(3) *My tutor was middle-aged, with a young wife.* This was the Revd. Charles John Myers, scholar of Trinity College, Cambridge and in 1823 fifth wrangler; Vicar of Flintham from 1829 to 1870. He married Mary Caroline, daughter of S. Broomhead Wood of Mount Pleasant, Sheffield and in 1827 he published *An Elementary Treatise on the Differential Calculus.*

CHAPTER II

(1) *A distant cousin.* He was Colonel Thomas Blackborne Thoroton, later Thoroton Hildyard, Coldstream Guards.

(2) *Of the three boys &c.* The actual careers differed slightly from those given in the text as intended. The eldest entered the Rifle Brigade, the second became a parson and the third a J.P., Yorks. (East Riding). The Hildyard seat in Holderness was Winestead.

(3) *The maiden aunt* was Mary Isabella Thoroton, (b. 1775), daughter of Thomas Thoroton, M.P., of Screveton Hall.

(4) *A clergyman and the best rider to hounds in the county.* See Chapter IV, note 1.

CHAPTER III

(1) *Mr——.* Crawshay published this anonymously.

CHAPTER IV

(1) *The pack was famous and so was the Master.* Identification has unexpectedly proved not quite certain. Baily's *Hunting Directory* and the Victoria County History shew that from 1827 to 1835 and again from 1840 to 1845 the Master was John Musters and that in the interval the Master was first Lord Middleton and then Mr Dansey. The latter's age I do not know but Lord Middleton was born in 1769. Which of the two was Master in the season here relevant, namely that of 1838 to 1839, remains uncertain. I am grateful to the present Joint-Master, Major George Vallance, to Major Robert Chaworth-Musters and to Mr Myles Hildyard for their help in this matter. The Hunt is the South Notts. It also remains uncertain who was the hunting parson described as 'the best rider to hounds in the county' and equally famed for his skill in breaking horses to the hunting field, which is a pity; he was clearly a character and one would like to identify him.

(2) *My father had two houses.* That in the country was at Colney Hatch, that in London was presumably that in Montague Street (No. 1, if I remember correctly) which in 1880, when my father was born there, belonged to George Crawshay. By an odd chance it backs on to the north-eastern corner of the British Museum of which my father, who joined the staff in 1903, eventually became Secretary.

CHAPTER V

(1) *The very good school.* This was a private school at North End House, Hampstead. The head master was a Dr. Evans, a great friend of Thomas Campbell the poet, whose visits Crawshay remembered with pleasure. Another visitor was Czartoryski the Polish exile.

(2) *A tragic end in Abyssinia.* This may well have been Walter C. Plowden, the British Consul murdered there in 1860 with his friend J. T. Bell, an engineer.

(3) *An old pocket book.* This does not survive.

(4) The market town is Newark,

(5) I am informed by Mr Myles Hildyard that Nanny Thorpe's cottage no longer exists. Nor does the mill.

(6) *The charm of running water.* The river is the Trent. At the beginning of the notebook in which Crawshay pasted the printed text of *A Silver Shape* some manuscript verses include one beginning:

> When heaviness my heart opprest,
> Nor would my brain, though weary, rest,
> I fled, sweet river, unto thee,
> For oh! thou wast a friend to me.
>
> A soothing friend of look serene
> And dear companion hast thou been
> To wander on with side by side
> Through fields & woods at even-tide.

And so on—not verse of a more than mediocre standard, but it corroborates the text and in the last couplet he describes himself as being there

> Alive to nothing but the sense
> Of thy serenest influence.

CHAPTER VII

(1) *A gentleman called.* 'An uncle,' says George Crawshay, 'of my young friends' but not, I gather from Mr Myles Hildyard, a Hildyard or a Thoroton. He was possibly related on the distaff side (and of course after half a century George Crawshay may have misremembered the precise relationship). 'Bessy's' mother's maiden surname was Whyte; but here again Mr Hildyard is at a loss. 'Bessy's' grandmother was the Hildyard heiress.

CHAPTER VIII

(1) Another of the manuscript verses mentioned is entitled 'To the Violet' and begins:

The violet blooms in the woodland dell,
But it bloometh not for me.

CHAPTER IX

(1) *A visit to some relatives there.* Probably these were his sister Constance and her husband Frank Stanley who had married on 24 April 1838.

CHAPTER X

(1) The distant view is southward over the Vale to Belvoir in the distance.
(2) *A great scholar and most amiable gentleman.* Not identified.
(3) *Another pupil.* Not identified
(4) *A very singular and interesting character.* This was William Sidney Walker (1795–1846).
(5) *His valuable commentaries on Shakespeare were published after his death*—at Crawshay's expense. See also the postscript.
(6) *Taglioni.* Maria Taglioni (1804–1884), in her day an internationally famous ballet dancer, born in Stockholm, where her father was ballet-master.
(7) *A young baronet.* Sir John Charles Thorold of Syston near Grantham, 11th Baronet. They married on 17 March 1841.

CHAPTER XI

(1) The manuscript journal of these travels, which I have, does not contain the passage here quoted but only the words 'he told me a piece of news which so disturbed my mind that I saw nothing more', the date 8 May 1843 being identical. Presumably Crawshay made a fair copy and destroyed the original.
(2) The landed estate which Crawshay acquired was that of Haughton Castle on the north Tyne. The Castle until he improved and enlarged it was medieval in fact and in one respect at least its character had yet to progress into the nineteenth century. My grandmother in old age recalled that when she was a girl of eleven or twelve a footman, if the weather were bad, would wait in the hall after breakfast bearing an umbrella, escort her down the garden path, wait outside and escort her back! Correcting

'BESSY' IN 1856, THEN LADY THOROLD

From a portrait by Edmund Havell the younger (b.1819) in the possession of Myles T. Hildyard Esq.

this item of domestic routine was one of George Crawshay's improvements. His architect was Salvin, whose northern blood—the Salvins had long been established in county Durham—combined with professional skill particularly fitted him for such work in Northumberland, where his restoration of Alnwick Castle is his most prominent but not his only memorial.

(3) George Crawshay's elder son Arthur (George Dufaud) went from Eton to Oriel College, Oxford and afterwards joined the staff of *The Rod and Gun* (since incorporated in *The Field*) mainly, I believe, as angling correspondent but also writing about shooting and hunting. The younger son, Martin, went from Harrow to his father's college at Cambridge but was not strong and settled in France, in or near St Malo.

(4) *Lady D——*; i.e. Lady Thorold. It is typical of Crawshay's delicacy that having for once preceded a blank name with an initial he chose to use an initial which merely approximates to the true one.

POSTSCRIPT

(1) Cf. Le Mallier, *Le Roman des Dufaud* (p. 113) on William Crawshay II. *'Il était comme son père, comme son grand-père l'avait été, un maître juste, exigeant pour le travail mais généreux envers qui le servait bien. Ne se contentant pas des rapports de ses contre-maîtres, il demeurait accessible au plus humbles de ses ouvriers, connaissant personellement chaque famille ouvrière et se souciant de leurs intérêts comme des siens.'*

William Crawshay II shot and fished but was ahead of his time in championing the otter. Mme Le Mallier (*op. cit.*, p. 112) records: *'J'ai horreur de cette chasse' déclara-t-il. 'J'aime les loutres; ce sont de nobles bêtes, intéressantes. Si un jour j'arrive à posséder de grandes terres au bord de l'eau, j'interdirai que le chasse traverse mon domaine. Les loutres auront un réfuge chez moi'*. In a footnote it is added that there is no evidence either way to shew whether he realised this aim or not but that a descendant, Robert Sandeman, protects the otter in his stretch of the same river, the Usk.

(2) For Sir John Fife see *The D.N.B.*

(3) Clive Newcome's words were these: 'I can't tell you what it is, or how it is, only one can't help seeing the difference. It isn't rank and that; only somehow there are some men gentlemen and some not, and some women ladies and some not.'

(4) For David Urquhart see *The D.N.B.*

(5) The quotation 'He would be very free &c.' is taken from the history of Hertfordshire by Sir Henry Chauncy (1632–1719) and is repeated by all subsequent historians of the county, rightly unable to resist so attractive a sentence.

(6) Genealogically this is not in every case exact; no matter. The need in this context is to supply a convenient phrase indicating the lapse of time.

N.B. The editor hopes that he may be forgiven for adding that the surname Hildyard is to be pronounced 'Hillyard' and that in the surnames Thoroton and Thorold the first syllable is to be pronounced as in 'thorough'.

Acknowledgments

Mr Esdaile and the publisher wish to thank the present editor and the proprietors of *The Newcastle Chronicle*, in which the narrative first appeared in serial form, for their permission to reproduce the text and also the pen drawing of George Crawshay. Thanks are also extended to Major George Vallance, M.F.H., Mr Myles Hildyard and to Major Robert Chaworth-Musters for their help in annotating the hunting episodes. Mr Esdaile's sketches which are intended to portray scenes familiar to 'Bessy' Hildyard and George Crawshay are based not only on those existing scenes which remain often almost unchanged since Queen Victoria's coronation, but also on documents made freely available for this purpose by Mr Hildyard of Flintham Hall who also supplied the charming portrait of 'Bessy'. Although the stableyard and the Rectory (in fact Vicarage; Crawshay, writing long after, has clearly misremembered) remain as they were in 1838, the church was restored in the 1890's, with effects on its external appearance. The Hall was rebuilt some thirty years earlier in a neo-Venetian style, at variance with the rebuilding of 1798. Finally, the editor wishes to thank Mrs Pamela Brown for help with the typing and to acknowledge his own family's forbearance whilst confined by a *milieu* of papers.